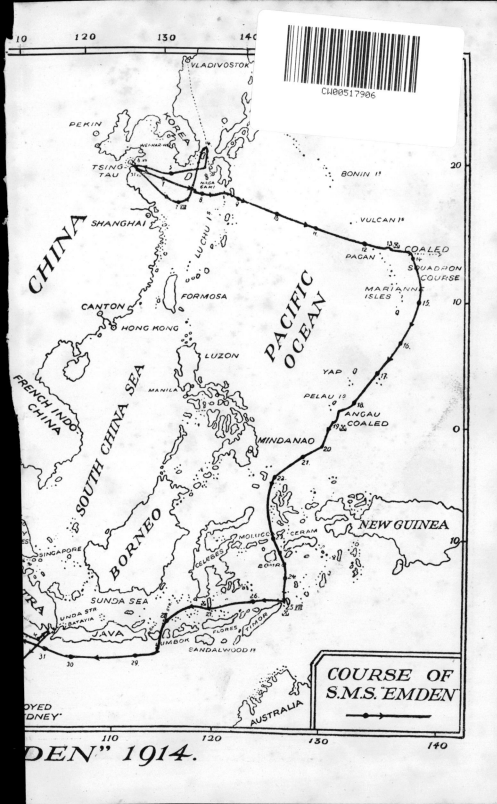

COURSE OF
S.M.S. "EMDEN

"EMDEN" 1914.

G. Lewis Day.
The Old Redoubt
Houghton — Hunts:
March 17th 1937

EMDEN

Eighth Printing
(Popular Edition)

Printed in Great Britain by Lowe & Brydone (Printers) Ltd., London N.W.1.

PUBLISHER'S NOTE

This is an epic of adventure, and as clear and circumstantial as any of the daring voyages recorded by Hakluyt. Indeed, it recalls to an Englishman the exploits of those gallant " sea-dogs," Drake and Hawkins. The hero of this story is Captain von Müller—captain of the world-famous raiding cruiser *Emden*—a foe so worthy that the English Government wished to honour him, after the war. There were, however, difficulties in the way. The Captain has been dead long since, but his spirit lives on in these stirring pages. The book is written by Franz Joseph, Prince of Hohenzollern, and is now translated for the first time into English.

The volume has had an enormous sale in Germany. But it is not a book for Germans only. It is a book to be read by all who admire courage and daring, by all who delight in the thrill of adventure ; by all who love true sportsmanship.

FOREWORD

THE activities of the *Emden*, during the year of the war, 1914, set the whole world, friend and foe, wondering, and innumerable pens in motion.

Most of this unauthorised *Emden* literature is, however, more zealous than accurate, and it may be truthfully said that it leaves legitimate demands unsatisfied, and an exact and connected description of all the events that happened is conspicuously absent.

Our commanding officer, the unforgettable and heroic Kapitän von Müller, never wrote a line about himself or the *Emden*. The first officer, Kapitän-leutnant von Mücke, in his report, dealt with the activities of the ship and ship's company, during the time he was on board the *Emden*. He was in command of the landing-party for the destruction of a cable and wireless station, and never saw the *Emden* again. He bravely escaped on the *Ayesha*, and made his return by the land route, through Palestine, Syria, etc.

The official Admiralty publication necessarily treats the activities of the *Emden* with brevity, and offers only a survey of the outstanding features. Many of my heroic ship-mates wrote their own experiences in detail, and these are scattered in periodicals and hard to come by. The outcry about the enormous amount of "literature" on the *Emden* is unwarranted; for this "literature" consists entirely of romantically embellished fantasies, stories for schoolboys, written in war time by laymen, founded on newspaper reports and naturally possessing no resemblance to truth.

I served as second torpedo officer in the *Emden* from the beginning of her activities to the destruction of the ship, and was then, with Kapitän von Müller and the rest of the survivors, interned for five years at Malta as a prisoner of war.

In this book I give an exact and connected account of all the activities of the *Emden*, and dedicate it to the memory of our commanding officer, Kapitän z. S. von Müller, though dead, immortal in memory, and to our heroic dead.

For the truth of this account, I engage my hand and heart.

FRANZ JOSEPH, PRINZ VON HOHENZOLLERN,

Oberleutnant z. S. a. D.

CONTENTS

EMDEN

EMDEN

CHAPTER I

ON June 29th, 1914, there reached us, in Tsingtau, the fateful telegram saying that the
Archduke Francis Ferdinand of Austria,
the heir to the throne, and his consort the Duchess
of Hohenberg, had been murdered in Sarajevo.
None of us immediately thought of a European
conflict. None the less most of us held the opinion
that Austria-Hungary would not put up with this
outrage from the Serbs without compensation.
We naturally spent the succeeding days in constant
suspense, and fell eagerly upon the dispatches
from home as they came in. At the same time we
lived peaceably at Tsingtau, and without a thought
of war.

We carried out our exercises both in the gunnery
and torpedo sections. The new hands had to be
thoroughly trained, and made familiar with every
branch of their duty.

For us officers those weeks were full of variety.
Bathing was in full swing, and we practised swimming whole-heartedly. The time was also en-
livened by entertainment between individual
friends ; we were much invited out, and organised

cheerful parties on board in return, which had a charming setting in the summer weather.

Our original intention was to proceed during the course of July to Shanghai, and thence to the Yangtsekiang as guard-ship. Those of us who did not yet know the Yangtse, that is the majority, were pleased at the prospect of getting to know a new district and new places. On July 7th, however, a stroke was ruled across this reckoning, for we received orders to remain at Tsingtau provisionally as guard-ship. At this news, so unaccountable did it seem, we were at first aghast ; it was obvious that the higher authorities did not regard the political situation as altogether free from danger.

Naturally, during those days there were also more service duties than usual. The evolutions of "Action stations" and "Clear ship for Action" were now frequently on the orders of the day. The whole ship's company had to be brought into such a condition that they should at any time be fit to go into action. This was indeed always the case, but the new hands needed more work, as they had not yet had sufficient experience. Only by repeated evolutions and practical experience could this be quickly and certainly brought about.

In the middle of our work a new element of surprise appeared, which also gave us to think. On the afternoon of July 22nd the Austro-Hungarian cruiser, *Kaiserin Elizabeth*, appeared at

Tsingtau. It was as clear as day that this was no mere act of courtesy. Our ally was seeking shelter and support in the presence of a friendly ship. In particular she was frightened of the hostile power of the Russian fleet, for Russia had always played patron to all the Slav states and had a corresponding influence over the policy of these countries. Austria-Hungary had from time immemorial been a brake on the " Greater Russia " policy ; and it therefore seemed extremely likely that Russia would willingly have seen this obstacle removed. It was quite possible that the political situation in the Balkans would give Russia an easy opportunity for interference. If this conclusion was justified, another question became imminent.

The arrival of our ally in Tsingtau made further occasion for festivities, which naturally took on a very hearty character. There were many exchanges of hospitality between the *Emden* and the cruiser *Kaiserin Elizabeth*. Very friendly relations were soon established between the officers of the two ships. We made motor expeditions to the Laushan Mountains and to Mecklenburg House, and various excursions in the beautiful country surrounding Tsingtau. The garrison also gave musical dinners and other entertainments.

At the same time we did not lose sight of the development of the political situation. Our commanding officer Kapitän von Müller, and his faithful officer, Leutnant von Guérard, were in constant communication both with the squadron, which was in the South Seas, and also with the naval higher command in Berlin. This was an extremely important matter, for we also acted partly as a relay station for news from home for the cruiser squadron.

The political situation continued to draw to a head. Serbia, supported by Russia, maintained her stand against Austria, who had sent an ultimatum. Germany's attitude was one of standing by, with a view to helping in case Russia should attack.

On July 29th we received the news that Austria-Hungary had declared war on Serbia. If indeed there was as yet no " pressing danger of war " for Germany, it was still the duty of our commanding officer, as senior officer of the Eastern Asiatic station in the absence of the Squadron Commander-in-Chief, to prepare for possible war by mobilising all the resources of the station for the outfit and maintenance of the cruiser squadron.

On the night before July 30th our commanding officer received a telegram from the Admiralty staff, informing him of a further approach to a crisis in the political situation. A council was therefore held on the 30th, on board the *Emden*, of all commanding officers present in Tsingtau. This council promulgated the following orders: (1) The fitting out of the collier *Elsbeth*, chartered for the South Seas cruise of the cruiser squadron, to be completed with all dispatch. She is to be sent to Yag. (2) The completion of repairs to the *Kormoran* to be carried on as quickly as possible. (3) The organisation of the Tsingtau base to be carried on under the commanding officer of the *Iltis*, Korvettenkapitän Sachse. (4) The navigating officer of the *Tiger*, Oberleutnant zur See Baumaken, owing to imminent danger of war, to be transferred to Batavia as base officer. (5) *Jaguar*, *Luchs*, and torpedo-boat *S*.90, to be placed at the disposal of the government of Tsingtau for the maintenance of security. (6) The commanding officer, *Jaguar*, Korvettenkapitän Luring, at present in Shanghai, to proceed with the organisation of the Shanghai base for China. (7) The order was laid down in which the guard of gunboats should be drawn on for attendance on the auxiliary cruisers.

We also were not idle at that time, but occupied in unloading all articles coming under " Paragraph A." These were principally all things that did not appear to be necessary in time of war, and especially all light inflammable articles, such as clothes, linen, things bought on the voyage, etc.

On the same day all officers were called into the cabin, where the Captain instructed us fully about the political situation. Further, in order to pass on telegrams more quickly, a party was told off for duty at the telegraph office.

On July 31st a telegram was received, announcing the beginning of political tension between the Central European Powers and the Triple Entente. At the same time our base received a communication from the Admiralty, according to which ten thousand tons of coal were to be shipped at the Tsingtau depot for the cruiser squadron. It was therefore a question of providing the necessary shipping. Our own ship received the order to land all articles coming under " Paragraph B " (carpets, curtains, wooden furniture, etc.). When one remembers all the things to be found in a cruiser on foreign station, one can form a rough picture of the work such an order must mean. The work was got through, however, almost like play. In addition all objects which could remain on board, but which might be dangerous in action either by splintering or burning, had to be got under the armoured deck. Though all worked willingly and keenly, this was still a severe task. Further, the gunnery officer claimed a part of the ship's company to take in ammunition. Provisions and coal had also to be provided. The coaling was carried out by Chinese from the dockyard. Our first officer, Kapitän-leutnant von Mücke, had work and worry to spare, enough in fact for several men. In the torpedo branch also war heads were to be taken in.

The *Kaiserin Elizabeth* had made fast alongside Mole No. 1 and was landing her fittings in the same way as ourselves. The steamer *Elsbeth* was filling her hold with coal, destined for the cruiser squadron. Meanwhile the garrison of Tsingtau also found occupation : parties of them were stationed to look after the things landed by us until they could be brought under cover in the dockyard.

We were now " clear," steam was got up in the boilers, the guns were provided with effective ammunition, and the torpedoes were fitted with war heads. All these were tasks which had to be done with the utmost exactitude. Lastly, those of the ship's company who were in the base hospital also came on board. We were now ready for action.

Our commanding officer had decided, in order to avoid a blockade by hostile warships, to sail on July 31st. We received his order to be clear for sea by seven o'clock. Punctually at seven we cast off from the coaling wharf of the Imperial Dockyard of Tsingtau, and steamed southwards, with the *Elsbeth*, whom we were to convoy part of her way.

We had scarcely left the harbour when the call, " Clear ship for Action," was given by drum and bugle. Great was our suspense ; we had to expect the appearance of hostile warships, attacking the ships leaving Tsingtau.

As nothing of this sort occurred we assumed that the alarm was a precautionary measure. Only later did we get certain news, that the Commander-in-Chief of the English East Asiatic squadron had

indeed intended to cruise in open formation outside Tsingtau, and capture or destroy any German
ship he met with. This possibility was imminent,
for at that time the English ships were lying at
Wei-hai-wei, the English protectorate north of
Tsingtau. What a rich prize the enemy would
have made may be recognised from the fact that
the greater part of the coal and provision ships
for the cruiser squadron had their base at Tsingtau.
Happily, we had in the First Lord of the Admiralty,
Churchill, an involuntary ally. He gave the order
for the English squadron to assemble in Hong-
Kong, and from there to proceed together southward against us. Besides this, it might have been
dangerous for us that the French squadron, which
consisted of the armoured cruisers *Montcalm* and
Duplex and a few torpedo boats, was going from
Vladivostock to Wei-hai-wei. There were, therefore, at that time a good number of hostile
ships about who could have made things very
unpleasant for us.

We remained unsighted, however, and steamed
southwards. At nightfall " War watches " were
set—that is, watches were set at the guns, searchlights, and torpedo tubes. The other watches
turned into their hammocks fully clothed, and
were, moreover, specially placed so that they
could reach their " Clear ship " stations quickly.
In these watches special look-outs were also
posted ; they were distributed between the positions on the masts, captain's bridge, and after-

super-structure, and were to give notice of any suspected ship, or whatever else there might be. Some of these posts were in charge of officers, so that a specially sharp supervision could be exercised. This kind of " War watches " we afterwards called " Full war watches," in opposition to " Light war watches," which were introduced during our voyages. It was very severe work for everybody, for there were only two watches, whereas otherwise the watches were divided into four.

Till eleven o'clock we accompanied the *Elsbeth* southwards, and then left her and laid our course for the island of Quelpart. It was intended that the cruise should be continued till we could obtain final news of the political situation. We were in close communication with the wireless station at Tsingtau.

The first night passed without disturbance, and on August 1st we also met nothing. Lively wireless conversation was, however, heard quite near, from which it could be gathered that English warships must be close to us.

A sharp look-out had to be kept. All mast-head look-outs were in the charge of officers. I was placed aft, which was no enjoyable position at high speeds, for one had continually in one's face the stream of " stokers "—that is, flakes of soot drawn up with the smoke out of the funnels. The horizon was, however, searched in vain for smoke or the masts of hostile ships.

We wished to get out of reach of the steamer track from Wei-hai-wei to Shanghai, and therefore steamed still farther eastwards. There was no special employment, because most of the ship's company was needed for the conversion of the ammunition from practice to effective conditions. Towards evening we received the wireless message that Germany had ordered the mobilisation of the whole army and the fleet.

Uncertainty was now at an end ; this news was synonymous with the outbreak of war. The excitement on board was naturally great. There could be no doubt that France and Russia were our enemies, but in our minds there was still some question as to whether England would join in.

August 2nd was a Sunday. First of all, the conversion of the ammunition was completed, and then Divine Service was held. After that the command was given, " Everybody aft," and the Captain made a speech in which he told us the news of the mobilisation, and emphasised that he expected from the ship's company the performance of their duty up to the last, so that after the war each one might be able to hold up a proud head before the War Lord. At the end, three cheers were given for " His Majesty the Emperor," in which all joined with enthusiasm. Afterwards there was a pause to allow the ship's company to rest from the strain, which had become really severe.

In the evening it was again " Full war watches,"
and at night naturally the same.

The morning of August 3rd brought the news of
the outbreak of war with Russia and of the immin-
ence of war with France. The time of waiting
was over.

Our Captain gave orders for a northerly course.
The *Emden* was to cut the Nagasaki-Vladivostock
shipping line, still avoiding enemy ships of war.
Our first object was to cripple enemy trade.
The ships on the chosen route were principally
Russian, and this was therefore our best field of
operations. First of all we made for the Straits
of Korea.

On August 4th, at about two in the morning,
during a very strong white squall we came up with
a ship, but could only see her stern-light. We did
not press farther forward, for it was possible that
we had to do with a French cruiser. Some French
warships were just then on their way to Wei-
hai-wei. We carried on and entered the Straits of
Tsushima in very bad weather and a very heavy
sea. I still lay peacefully in my berth when the
order, " Clear ship for Action," wakened all on
board. I hurried to my action station, which at
that time was in the conning-tower. The *Emden*
was hurrying full speed in chase of a cloud of
smoke. Soon the masts and the stern of the ship
came in view. Above them were the mast-head
flags.

Was this a hostile warship or not? On a

closer view we soon made out that we had to do with a very speedy Russian passenger ship, which was using all speed to escape into neutral waters.

The *Emden* fired a warning round which was disregarded by the Russian.

Thereupon we fired a few rounds across her bow, of which the last went so close to the Russian, that the captain probably became very anxious and troubled, for he turned his ship about and stopped. At the same time, however, he tried to give the S.O.S. signal by wireless, and give his name.

Naturally the Russian was roundly interrupted in this effort by a wireless message from us, and finally captured in Latitude 35° 5′ N., Longitude 19° 39′ E. The ship was the *Rjäsan*, one of the Russian volunteer fleet, built at the Schichau dockyard and still fairly new. Her cargo was small in proportion ; but the Russian had eighty passengers on board who showed great anger at the original hardy attitude of the captain, for the shells had gone very close to them.

The sending of a prize crew under Oberleutnant z. S. d. R. Lauterbach turned out to be dangerous at least for some moments. The boat was lowered into the water and the prize crew had to transfer themselves on board the *Rjäsan*. Owing to the very heavy sea the boat was nearly stove in under the ladder, in going alongside. For assistance and security the second life-boat was piped away. Luckily an accident was avoided.

When everything was secure in the captured ship, the *Rjäsan* was ordered to follow the *Emden*. It was our Captain's intention to bring the prize to Tsingtau and convert her, as she had sufficient command of speed, into an auxiliary cruiser. We now wheeled about and laid our course for Tsingtau.

The morning passed quietly, and we did not meet any ships. In the *Rjäsan* something seemed to be out of order, or some difficulties were found. Perhaps, encouraged by the captain, the Russians were trying to strike. Our Captain sent a message to the captain of the *Rjäsan* letting him know that the *Rjäsan* was now our prize and was therefore subject to German martial law. The Russian understood this at once and became docile.

On board the *Rjäsan* Oberleutnant Lauterbach, according to his duty as captain of the prize, had inspected the wireless log-book and made out from it that the Russian, both this morning an during her voyage, had been in communication with French ships. Naturally he informed the *Emden* of this, and was given instructions in case of a meeting with hostile ships to try to proceed separately to Tsingtau. If this were impossible the *Rjäsan* was to be sunk. As to us in the *Emden*, to make our watch as sharp as possible a signalman was sent aloft as look-out in

the foremost crow's nest. On our later voyages
this was done regularly and at all times, as the
visibility is much greater from aloft than from
the bridge.

At about three o'clock in the afternoon we met
with a Japanese fishing steamer, which we left
undisturbed. It might have been five or half-
past when the look-out reported the smoke of
about five ships on the starboard bow. A little
later the smoke could also be seen from the
bridge ; the crow's nest had the masts already in
sight.

We now knew where the French squadron was
to be found. We were then south of the Island
of Tsushima ; the Frenchmen were in all probability the cruisers *Montcalm* and *Duplex* with a
few destroyers, and the squadron must have
passed through the west canal of the Straits of
Tsushima and be now on their way to Shanghai.

The *Emden* had no wish to fall into the arms
of the French. Our Captain therefore gave the
order for an easterly course and only when darkness had fallen did we slowly return through
N.N.W. to our former westerly direction. The
Rjäsan, with everything clear for sinking, followed the *Emden*.

As usual it was war watches that night. We
met no steamers or other vessels but were forced
to observe that on board the Russian the complete " black-out " (steaming with lights hidden)
was not functioning properly. Several times

we had to use our Morse lantern to make our
people aware of the failure and request them to
remedy it.

The *Emden* laid her course for Tsingtau and
passed between the Island of Quelpart and the
Korean Peninsula.

On August 5th at about twelve noon we came
upon two big Japanese ships, who dipped their
flags to us and were answered with equal courtesy
by the *Emden*. In the afternoon we again
sighted smoke clouds which we gave place to for
the sake of prudence. In the evening we heard by
wireless that England also had declared war on
Germany ; the *Emden* could now act with freedom. We had enemies enough, God knows, but
we were still cheerful, for everyone in the *Emden*
knew that much could be endured with such a
ship's company. It could only be of advantage
to us that we need have no further consideration
for England. We could now hope for rich booty
in the war on merchant shipping, for English
shipping was the most plentiful of all in the East.

We had now to be doubly alert, for it was
possible, indeed probable, that English war-ships
would be lying in wait before Tsingtau to capture
any ships entering or leaving the harbour. It
was imperative for us, on account of our valuable
prize, to try, under whatever circumstances, to
reach Tsingtau in company with the *Rjäsan*.

Our Captain was determined to bring this
about. To make sure, we asked Tsingtau by

wireless whether enemy war-ships had been sighted. The answer was in the negative. The *Emden* had now to get " home " to Tsingtau, for she needed coal and also had to take on board the prescribed reserves of officers and men.

Till now the *Rjäsan* had preceded the *Emden*, as it was considered desirable to have the Russian under close observation, but now on the voyage " home " she had to be astern of us, so that in the case of an encounter with an enemy the prize ship, under command of Lauterbach, should be able to try to escape, or if this was not successful, to run herself aground.

On approaching Tsingtau the order for " clear ship " was given, and all boilers had steam up for full speed.

Very lively wireless conversations could be heard by the *Emden*, and we could tell from the strength of the sound that the enemy must be near us.

We set our course first for the Cha-lien-tao lighthouse, which stood on an island protecting the bay of Tsingtau, and then for Cape Yatau. Towards three o'clock a ship was sighted with a very bright stern light.

The suspense on the bridge of the *Emden* grew. It was believed that we had an enemy vessel before us. Many eyes tried to pierce the night, but they could discover nothing decisive.

On our course along the high and rocky coast a cry of " Alarm " suddenly rang out, and was

almost at once repeated. The suspense was now
at its highest. We had not, however, as we supposed, enemy destroyers before us, but only
peaceful Chinese junks.

In the grey of the morning the mine barrier
was reached, and near it we met the German ship
C.S. Leiss, which was waiting to be allowed to
enter. In Tsingtau everything was already in a
state of war. No light was burning, and the once
well-lighted town was in complete darkness,
looking like a deserted town after a siege.

Near the Island of Maitau the *Emden* gave a
signal, which was at once answered by the blaze
of the so-called " Entry gun." We had announced our arrival by wireless, and everything
was therefore prepared for us, and ran smoothly.
The *Jaguar* was lying outside the mine barrier,
and at once sent a steamboat across to us. Kapitänleutnant von Saldern, the captain of the boom,
and an old friend of ours, Matthiessen the pilot,
came aboard and took the *Emden* safely through
the entrance. The prize, *Rjäsan*, had followed
us faithfully, but could not come in at once, and
had to wait outside the barrier.

Between five and six in the morning the *Emden*
entered the harbour, where for greater safety
there was a boom of chains and timber, and made
fast at the coaling mole. The mole-head was
already guarded by guns and men of the marine
artillery. We were received by many officers
including the captain of the *Kormoran*, and the

latter inquired anxiously after the speed of our prize. He hoped that the *Rjäsan* could be fitted out as an auxiliary cruiser, for the *Kormoran* was an old cruiser, and so out of condition that she could no longer be used as a sea-going war-ship. The hope of the *Kormoran's* captain was shortly realised.

CHAPTER II

THE *Emden* was to coal as quickly as possible up to 950 tons, leave harbour again in the evening and join the squadron on August 10th, when they would be anchored at Pagan, an island of the Marianne group. We had therefore to make haste and take in at the same time some equipment which we lacked and also put ashore some unnecessary articles. To bring our ship's company up to war strength we took on three more officers, one deck officer (Deckoffizier), seventeen seamen, and thirteen technical petty officers and men. In addition we took on board one Catholic priest so that the Catholics could receive the sacraments and general absolution. We had not much time for this, but we succeeded in doing it all, and the work was done cheerfully. We received many visits from Tsingtau. People wished to see the ship after the first war-time cruise and to hear our accounts, for the most blood and thunder stories were told about us, among others that we had sunk the Russian cruiser *Askold* in fair fight. Acquaintances and friends wished to take leave, for no one knew if we should meet again.

As we have said, there were guns and guards

on the mole, but the big floating dock had also been made clear for sinking. Most of the ships lying at the mole were fully loaded and only waiting for the order to leave, and among them was the *Prince Eitel Friedrich* of the Norddeutscher Lloyd, which had been fitted out as an auxiliary cruiser. The *Markomannia* of the Hamburg America line had been ordered to accompany us under the command of her captain, Kapitän Fahss, and was lying clear for departure.

At about six o'clock the Captain reported the *Emden* clear, and soon afterwards we left amid the cheers of those left behind, and accompanied by torpedo boat *S*.90, which was accompanying us to Cape Yatau to see all clear, by the auxiliary cruiser *Prinz Eitel Friedrich*, and by the *Markomannia*.

At the outer roads we again anchored for a short time, and our Captain went over to the *Markomannia* for a conference. When he returned we were piloted through the mine barrier and proceeded out to sea on the course of the steamship line from Yokohama to Shanghai.

The night passed without disturbance.

On August 7th the work was made as light as possible so that the ship's company could recover from their recent severe efforts.

That night the *Markomannia* and the *Eitel Friedrich* took the first steps in a colossal masquerade. The former was given the markings of a Blue Funnel liner and the *Prinz Eitel Friedrich*, according to her degree, took those of the more distinguished P. & O. line. This meant a great deal of work, for to repaint a large ship is no bagatelle.

The *Markomannia* lacked especially the larger funnel which is a characteristic of the Blue Funnel liners.

In the forenoon of August 8th we sighted a smoke cloud, which we at once approached at full speed. Our companions maintained their old course and speed. In the *Emden* there was no little curiosity as to what we should discover. Our expectations were disappointed, for the eagerly expected enemy was a Japanese of the Nippon Yusen Kaisha, and therefore a neutral. Nothing was left for us after this disappointment but to put a good face on bad fortune and return to our companions.

On the same day the *Markomannia* was sent in advance on account of her lower speed, with the order to pass the Japanese Lu-chu Islands and to meet the *Emden* S.E. of them.

We then cruised with the *Eitel Friedrich* along the steamer route between Nagasaki and Shanghai, in the hope of coming by some fatted morsel. We had not, however, much time for this, as we had soon to meet the squadron at Pagan.

In the afternoon we sighted a steamship and gave chase, but again it was a Japanese. The luck was not in our favour, and at the beginning of twilight we left this hunting ground and steamed with the *Eitel Friedrich* in the Colnett Straits, between the Lu-chu Islands.

In the evening we received, for the first time since leaving Tsingtau, exact wireless messages about the situation in the European theatre. It was good news, of successful battles in Belgium, and stout resistance presented to the Russians in East Prussia. Also, of the greatest interest to us, there was good news of the navy. The well-known pleasure steamer, the *Konigin Luise*, had sown mines in the Thames with good results, but was, however, overwhelmed by hostile war-ships, and sunk. This price did not seem too high, on the other hand, as the little English cruiser, the *Amphion*, ran on to the mines and sank. Also our two ships *Goeben* and *Breslau*, in spite of being surrounded by many enemies, had succeeded in passing through the Straits of Messina and escaping.

At this news of our comrades at home we were naturally very proud, and saw in it the results of the energetic and comprehensive training which had been given to our navy.

That evening we intercepted a wireless message concerning ourselves, in which it was broadcasted that the *Emden* was then in the Eastern Sea with two captured steamships. It was easy to guess who was to be thanked for this, for it could only be one of the Japanese ships that we had met, which must have broadcasted our position and warned our enemies.

One other piece of news we received that evening, which was that the English ship *Empress of Japan*, of the Canadian Pacific line, was on her way to Hong-Kong, and would be passing the South Japanese coast. As we had been cruising since the fall of darkness in the Colnett Straits, through which the liner must pass, we were bound to meet her. Punctually to our expectations, at nine o'clock the look-out announced a steamship. We were after her like a fox. At the right range the searchlight blazed out, but there was weeping and lamentation in the *Emden* when it disclosed another confounded Japanese. How we cursed needs no saying; but bad words could not mend matters. The searchlight was withdrawn, and we continued our former course in the darkness of night. Our lucky hour had certainly not struck yet.

August 9th, a Sunday, was kept, as far as possible, as a day of rest. After Divine Service, the ship's company scattered themselves over about the decks, and talked, or played cards. The Captain also joined us in the wardroom. In ideal weather, with a sea like a mirror, and the sky a splendid blue, there could be nothing better than to sit dozing on the quarter-deck, and rest. Our first officer, Kapitänleutnant von Mücke, wished, however, to use this time for the benefit of the ship's company, and explained to them the events in the European theatre of war, with the help of a large map. This was repeated every Sunday in

August, and later, when it was possible, every Sunday after Divine Service. The more intelligent men appreciated these lectures greatly, however sparing might be the news we received by wireless.

August 10th was a *dies iræ* in the truest sense of the word. The last remains of the amenities of a warship had to be sacrificed, under this head being the small amount of upholstery and the rest of the wood panelling in the wardroom. Away with comfort and all its works! A sailor's heart is indeed not set upon tinsel and show, but nevertheless some of our officers were filled with regrets that the wardroom, which had hitherto been a well-appointed room with some attraction about it, should be turned into nothing but a cold, dank " flat," with nothing comfortable or homely about it ; indeed, very depressing There was some consolation to be found in the fact that it was war that made these sacrifices necessary, and overboard went everything in the way of curtains, the screen between the wardroom and the after battery, and the remaining lockers in the officers' cabins. It had to be. The wardroom, however, must still be fit for human habitation, and the bulkheads were therefore covered with a poisonous green paint. The human race can adapt itself to anything.

The news received that evening by wireless was not cheerful. It was reported, more or less clearly, that England's ally, Japan, was apparently abandoning her neutral attitude, and would take active steps against German ships, if England's interests in China were attacked by Germany, or if Japanese shipping suffered any damage from the activities of the German navy.

The most unpleasant part of all for us was the news that the Japanese cruiser *Tone* and four destroyers had left Japan in a southerly direction. If Japan did indeed intend to take measures against German ships, our present course was severely threatened. Though there was no immediate danger, the greatest caution was required of us. We met the *Eitel Friedrich* at the appointed spot. On the other hand, the *Markomannia* was missing, which aroused great anxiety in the *Emden*. An attempt was therefore made to communicate with the vanished *Markomannia* by wireless, but without success. No answer was received.

On August 11th we acted as target tug for the *Eitel Friedrich*, who was breaking-in her guns. As there was still nothing to be seen or heard of the *Markomannia*, we again called her up by wireless.

This time we did receive an answer, which seemed peculiar and enigmatic: " Am at the rendezvous. Give your position."

What did this message mean, and what was intended ? The *Markomannia* had no need to know our position.

The *Emden* became a council chamber in which

the pessimists expressed their opinion that the *Markomannia* had been captured by some enemy, and that this enemy had sent the message hoping to find out the position of the *Emden*.

In order to make sure the *Emden* called the squadron, but received only the order, "Do not wireless." This was still more remarkable. Our wireless telegraphist said that both answers had been given with the same strength, and we therefore thought that the first answer must have come from the *Scharnhorst*, but we knew nothing certain. We were in great suspense and wholeheartedly anxious for the answer to our riddle. We were also concerned about the vanished ship.

However great our suspense, it made no difference to our duties. The Gunnery Officer therefore held a much-needed practice for his men with a short range target. Our steam pinnace towed a target float upon which hung in gimbals a metal plate of about six to eight square inches. A specially constructed rifle was then fixed into the guns and shooting practice could thus be held with ordinary rifle ammunition. This was particularly good practice for the gunlayers and numbers 1 (the latter being the reserve men, specially trained to take, if necessary, the place of the gunlayer). It was thus possible to keep the guns' crews in practice without too great an outlay, though only in favourable weather, for in any sea this method was rendered useless by the unsteadiness of the target.

Otherwise in the *Emden* the day passed quietly.
We were to arrive at Pagan on August 12th.
At half-past twelve some of the Marianne Islands
were already in sight, and a few of them we
passed. Then in the afternoon the Island of
Pagan came in sight at last, crowned by a volcano
of considerable height. The islands consist of a
range of mountains standing up out of the water.
Some time in pre-history this was a continent in
itself, with its own mountain ranges, and, perhaps
at the time of the Deluge, it sank, leaving as its
memorial only the peaks of the former mountains. Most of the islands are uninhabited, but
they were sought out by Japanese planters who
for the most part own cocoa and banana planta-
tions, looked after by the few original natives left.
Many of the islands are very fertile, owing to the
rich lava soil.

The companion ship of the squadron, the
Titania, was cruising outside Pagan Bay, and,
meeting us, hoisted her identification signal, to
which we replied. The *Emden* then turned to
starboard, and entered the bay, where everything
was looking very lively. Besides the armoured
cruisers *Scharnhorst* and *Gneisenau* and the little
cruiser *Nürnberg*, a great convoy of ships were
lying there, consisting of the *Prinz Waldemar*,
Holsatia, *Mark*, *York*, *Staatssekretär Krätke*, *Gouverneur Jäschke*, and *Longmoon*. We anchored fairly
well in. The other warships were already engaged
in coaling.

The *Emden* had scarcely anchored when our Captain received the order to proceed on board the flagship of Admiral Graf von Spee, and at the same time we received visitors. A barge came alongside from the *Gneisenau*, inquiring about mail, which, since we were not a mail steamer, we had not got on board.

In the Bay of Pagan we heard the news that those of my year had been promoted to Lieutenant's rank, which was good news for those of us who had joined the service in 1911, and had been studying for this object for some years. Our duties in the *Emden* were hardly altered, for we kept our former positions. In the evening the event was suitably celebrated.

The order for night watches was : " Men light war watches, officers full war watches."

August 13th was marked out for us by a particularly strenuous day's coaling. Lauterbach, who in peace-time was captain of the *Staatssekretär Krätke*, brought up his ship with her stern alongside us, and then the *Gouverneur Jäschke* on the starboard side. Coaling began at once, and the work was not by any means light.

With my division I had to look after the coaling in the *Staatssekretär Krätke*, and mightily we sweated over it, which was not surprising in the tropical heat. In addition the ships, which in peace-time plied as passenger ships between Shanghai, Tsingtau, and Port Arthur, were not properly equipped for coaling, particularly as regards the disposition of the holds. The work went slowly, but it still went on, even though the coal taken in by the *Emden* only amounted to 450 tons.

During this laborious day a very unpleasant discovery was made, which Lauterbach's quickness was able to turn to advantage. Like nearly all ships in the East, we had Chinese washermen, who were indispensable, for nobody could wash so well as they could. Our three washermen had heard from their countrymen in the other ships that this ship would return to Tsingtau. During coaling we discovered our three Chinese hidden in Lauterbach's ship, and they were, of course, brought back. To the demand that they should stay in the *Emden* and carry on their duties they returned an uncompromising negative. Their faces fell when they heard that no ship was to return to Tsingtau, and they abandoned their resistance. Unfortunately, all three were later killed by English shells.

During the heavy work of coaling we had no time to think about the fate of the vanished *Markomannia*. Our surprise was therefore the greater when at about nine in the morning she ran safely into the harbour of Pagan ; but who-ever had hoped to find out more about the experiences of her ship's company was deceived, for after the coaling was over we had to provision, which was particularly necessary for the *Emden*. After that we had a change of officers, exchanging

4

Kapitänleutnant d. R. Metzenthin, who was
already very senior, for Leutnants z. S. S. Gysling
and Roderich Schmidt, who later did the *Emden*
yeoman service as officers of prizes in the war
on merchant shipping.

In the morning a great consultation was held
in the *Scharnhorst*, in which all commanding
officers of cruisers took part, together with
Korvetten-kapitän Thierichens, Captain of the
auxiliary cruiser *Prince Eitel Friedrich*. The
latter was at that time in command of the convoy.

According to our Captain, the course of the
conference was as follows : The Squadron Commander-in-Chief gave his views of the situation
and the usefulness of the cruiser squadron. He
emphasised the threatening attitude adopted by
Japan, and the advantages of keeping the cruiser
squadron as long as possible in reserve. The
uncertainty about its position and aims would
occupy the attention of a great number of enemy
warships. He also spoke of the difficulties of
coaling, especially in regard to the big coal consumption of the *Scharnhorst* and *Gneisenau*. On
these grounds he had arrived at the decision to
proceed first with the squadron to the West coast
of America.

Commanding officers were then asked by the
Commander-in-Chief to give their opinion. I said
(Kapitän von Müller) that I was opposed to this
on the ground that during the several months'
voyage across the ocean the cruiser squadron

would be practically ineffective, that it could do the enemy no harm whatever, and that I attached great importance to the " fleet in being " theory, especially with regard to the future of the navy and our future sea power, which depended upon it. If the coaling difficulties were too great to permit the use of the squadron in East Asiatic, Australian, and Indian waters, I was bold enough to put forward for consideration the question whether it would not be right to send at least one of the smaller cruisers to the Indian Ocean. Conditions there would specially favour cruiser warfare, and the appearance of German warships on the Indian Coast would have a valuable influence for us on the morale of the Indian peoples. The Chief of Staff, Kapitän z. S. Fieltiz, and so far as I remember the other commanding officers as well, supported the idea of sending at least one small cruiser into the Indian Ocean. The Commander-in-Chief then stated that he had gone thoroughly into the question whether he should proceed to the Indian Ocean with the whole squadron, but had considered that it would be useless on account of the coaling difficulties. He would take into consideration the proposal to send a small cruiser, and if so the *Emden*, into the Indian Ocean. At the conference, the use of auxiliary cruisers was also discussed, and the Commander-in-Chief said that he did not place much reliance on such auxiliary cruisers as the *Prinz Eitel Friedrich* and the *Rjäsan* (*Kormoran*).

In his opinion their speed was not high enough, and they would also use up the coal provided for the cruiser squadron, which was already not too plentiful.

In conclusion the Commander-in-Chief stated his intention to leave Pagan that evening. All ships were to be clear for sea at 5.30 p.m.*

In the afternoon it was definitely decided that the *Emden* should be sent into the Indian Ocean, but, except the Captain, we heard nothing of it. It was an important decision for us, for we were now to be independent.

Punctually at five-thirty we weighed anchor, and in line ahead the squadron, followed by a long train of supply ships, swept out of the stillness of Pagan Bay. The *Scharnhorst* was leading, followed by the *Gneisenau*, *Nürnberg* and *Emden*. The *Titania* at the end brought up the first line. On the starboard quarter was the second line, with the *Eitel Friedrich* as leader, followed by the other ships in order of size. Good order was kept even by the commercial shipping, which was saying a great deal, for naturally they had had no practice in collective manœuvring. The course was east and the speed ten knots.

At nightfall full war watches were set. In the early morning the light showed us a terrible state of affairs. The warships were still in line ahead, but among the commercial shipping there was

---

* Extracts from :—" Der Kreuzerkrieg in den ausländische Gewässern" I. Bd. Das Kreuzerggschwader.

now no trace of proper station-keeping, and it took all the patience of the leaders to bring them into order again. No one can be blamed, however, for a merchant captain could not be expected to know better, being accustomed to steaming alone without reference to a leader. We slowed down, hoping that the missing ships would come up to us, but the smaller ships did not put in an appearance. We had to turn and go back on our course to look for them. In the end we found them all and were able to proceed on our course.

Our course was easterly and we believed that our destination was the West coast of America. This was actually one of the possibilities, for enemy trade was particularly lively between South America and Australia. A humanly-understandable hope also suggested the passage round Cape Horn, with the further possibility of returning home with the squadron.

At eight in the morning there was a great surprise for us in the *Emden* when the flagship ran up the signal: " *Emden* detached. Good luck."

In the whole ship there was great rejoicing and excitement. At last we were to be on our own and could act independently, as we, or our Captain, pleased. No sailor could ask more.

Our orders were to proceed independently, and act to the detriment of the enemy wherever it should be possible. Our Captain was the right man for such an undertaking.

Kapitän von Müller ordered the following signal to be sent to the Commander-in-Chief : " My dutiful thanks for the confidence placed in me. Success to the squadron and *bon voyage*."

Our companion ship, the *Markomannia*, received the order : " Follow the *Emden*." At the same time one of her signalmen was sent across to us, to ensure as far as possible that the understanding and general relations between the *Emden* and the *Markomannia* should be secured.

We then steamed S.S.W. at twelve knots, and were able to form some idea as to our destination. This course led directly to the East Indian archipelago. It was also, however, the way to the Indian Ocean.

CHAPTER III

THE squadron was soon out of sight. "Alone at last!" Alone! A word of much meaning for us! In the squadron one was always more or less a number in an organisation, but now the *Emden* was a fighting unit in her own right, and whoever knows naval life knows what that means. Every opportunity could be seized, and the credit for it would go to us. With good luck we could now make ourselves somebody, which is seldom the case in squadron warfare, where any laurels go to the central command.

Our course at first was southerly, running at a discreet distance parallel to the Marianne Islands. Our immediate goal was Angaur Island, of the Pelew Group, where we hoped to pick up a collier, which had been ordered to await us there, and take in further fuel. As soon as the Marianne Islands no longer stood in our way, our course was changed to S.W.

The voyage to Angaur lasted till August 19th, and we used the time to bring the ship still more into fighting trim. As stated, half of our ship's company were inexperienced, and the different fighting and engineering branches had therefore

to bring these men into a fully trained condition.
For example, the guns' crews, magazine crews
and range-finders received special training, in
which our companion, the *Markomannia*, served
us as a target.   In this she did us priceless service,
for range-finding and handling the guns could
not have been thought of without her.   Day by
day the men became visibly more at home with
their weapons.   This was not, however, our only
task.   Under the direction of the first officer the
protection of the *Emden* was added to.   Thus
the guns in the forecastle were masked by splinter
screens, consisting of interwoven hanks of hemp,
and the same was done to those under the quarter-
deck.   The after-gun control, the action station
of my friend and companion, Oberleutnant z. S.
von Levetzow, and the wireless room, which
stood between the second and third funnels, were
hung with matting, in the hope of protecting
them from splinters.   Unluckily it turned out,
in the final fight with the *Sydney*, that all these
precautions were useless, as the hemp and the
matting made rich material for the fire of
exploding shells.

In the torpedo branch the work was limited
to bringing the torpedoes into war condition,
as there was no time for shooting practice,
etc.

In the engineering branch there was also plenty
to do.   The boiler tubes had not improved with
use, but were easy to change, and exchanges and

repairs occupied the time in this department.   As
for the engines themselves, the work of keeping
them in running trim was sufficient.

In the disposition of the ship's company it
was arranged that the watch below should have
their sleeping places as close as possible to their
action stations.   At this time the men had always
light war watches, for it was necessary to allow
them sufficient time in the night to recuperate
after their very strenuous efforts during the day.
The principal difference between this and full
war watches was that a watch was only of two
hours' duration.   The torpedo personnel could not
be taken into account, for their work went on
continuously.   Men in the night watches had
extra rest by day, and also more food.   War
watches among the stokers were similarly
arranged.   As it was not possible to modify the
watches, compensation was made by way of extra
nourishment.

There was, of course, no respite for the officers.
With the best will in the world it could not have
been managed, as the number of posts commanded
by officers could not be reduced without endanger-
ing the ship.

The wireless staff was also not reduced at night
as this was the most favourable time for wireless.
Every evening regularly we received news from
Tsingtau of the position and events in the
different theatres.   I still remember, for instance,
how one evening the Adjutant, who was also

wireless officer, came running into the ward-room with the news, " four English warships have been sunk in the Humber by a night attack of German torpedo flotillas, and several more damaged." The rejoicing in the *Emden* may be imagined, and as our stock of wine was still plentiful and good the news was fittingly cele-brated. Unfortunately the message was later contradicted. Where it came from could not be discovered. Other news, however, which brought no rejoicing was also received, news which left no doubt that Japan would not hesitate much longer before joining Germany's enemies. The cause was, of course, Tsingtau. This protectorate, cherished by Germany with all possible care, awakened the jealousy of the Japanese, who afterwards tried to make Tsingtau, in their possession, a kind of second Gibraltar on Chinese soil. None of the Northern Chinese harbours were so up-to-date and well equipped as Tsingtau, and we had no doubt that Japan would seize the first opportunity to declare war against us. England, Japan's ally, was also naturally seeking relief in the East, in order to be able to limit her attention to Europe.

In the evening of August 19th the *Emden* was so near to the Pelew Islands that if the same speed be maintained the arrival at Angaur must have occurred that night. This was to be avoided, and the order was therefore given for slow speed. The principal reason for the order, however, was the wish to pass the Pelew Islands by daylight and keep a look-out for the collier which had been sent there. We did not know exactly whether she would be anchored in Angaur or at one of the other islands.

In the grey of the morning we came in sight of the islands. We ran past them at slow speed, but could see nothing of the collier we expected.

At eleven o'clock we reached Angaur, the southernmost island of the archipelago, and anchored in the northern roads. The island is not very large, but valuable on account of its phosphates. It was leased by a German company, which exploited the phosphates, and our arrival was therefore greeted by the German flag floating on the wind.

The *Markomannia* ran in and made fast to a buoy. We weighed anchor, went alongside her, and made all preparations for coaling, which in the tropics cannot be described as enjoyment.

Shortly after our arrival the manager of the phosphate company, who was also Government representative, and the doctor of the island, came on board to visit our Captain. Several other members of the German company also came out to the *Emden*, and were entertained by us in the wardroom. In spite of coal dust and other disadvantages the guests evidently felt at home with us, and were given refreshments. The Government representative asked specially whether we could give him any provisions. Some were gladly given, and others exchanged, but with all good will we could not spare very much.

We heard from this officer that three days before an English ship had left with 7,000 tons of phosphate on board, and our faces fell at the thought that such a valuable prize had escaped us.

The reserves on the island were told by the Captain that it would be impossible to take them as we had already our full complement. This afternoon we also expected a German mail steamer of the Norddeutscher Lloyd, the *Princess Alice*, who some days before had called the cruiser squadron by wireless but had not been answered. Our commanding officer, Kapitän von Müller, had thought it best to order her to Angaur. The message was sent, and we expected her between two and three o'clock. At two o'clock the signalman in the crow's-nest reported smoke clouds in a northerly direction. Shortly afterwards he was able to make out that it was a large black steamship with two yellow funnels, and was approaching the island.

The *Princess Alice* was a ship of ten thousand tons and therefore too large to anchor at the island. If she wished to remain stationary she had to manœuvre with her screws.

The Captain wished to go on board the *Princess Alice*, and we—that is, the Adjutant, the Schiffszahlmeister, the Marine-Oberzahlmeister, Woyschokowsky, and I—were to accompany him. As, however, the Adjutant had gone ashore to inspect the wireless station and give directions for further communication, we had to wait for his return.

I was glad of the opportunity of going on board the *Princess Alice,* for in this ship in 1913 I had taken the four weeks' voyage from Genoa to Shanghai which had brought me out to the East. The memory of that happy time made me glad to see her again.

On board the *Princess Alice* we were heartily greeted by all, the name of the *Emden* having become famous through the capture of the *Rjäsan.* Our Captain dealt with the question of reserves and then naturally asked for news. He was told that the *Princess Alice* on her journey out had taken over £850,000 sterling in gold for the Indian Government, to be delivered in Hong-Kong. Between Singapore and Hong-Kong the captain of the *Princess Alice* heard of the out-break of war, steamed full speed into the neutral American harbour of Manila, in the Philippines, and brought the gold into "safety." The English Government must have pulled a long face when they heard of their loss. In Manila the captain received instructions from the German consul to take in as much coal, provisions, and fresh water as she would hold and to join the German cruiser squadron. An attempt was made to join up, but it did not succeed as the right moment for it had passed.

The captain said that on August 7th an English squadron, consisting of the armoured cruisers *Minotaur* and *Hampshire* and the light cruiser *Yarmouth*, had appeared off the German island of Yap. The squadron commanding officer informed the wireless station there that within three hours they would be shot to pieces. When this had been done the squadron steamed away again without attempting a landing.

The most important news for us was that Japan had sent an ultimatum to Germany requesting the evacuation of Tsingtau by all military forces before September 5th. Japan requested an answer before August 23rd. It was clear to us in the *Emden* that no answer would be given by Germany, and the consequences we could imagine for ourselves.

This was not pleasant news for us, for we had now to reckon with Japan as a new enemy and our hearts were sore to think that Tsingtau, at the expiration of the time limit, would undoubtedly be attacked by Japan. Tsingtau would not be able to hold out, and it seemed that its fate was sealed.

We also received from the *Princess Alice* American newspapers whose contents were so imbecile that we could hardly believe them, consisting as they did of sensationalism and typically American Stock Exchange manœuvres.

While we were receiving the news the Zahl-meister was negotiating about provisions. With the same object our first officer came aboard the *Princess Alice* and hastened forward the conduct of affairs, but with very little result, for most of the time was wasted in the making out of requisition forms and receipts. " St. Bureau-cratius " was celebrated on board almost with orgies. The mail steamer's accountants lacked discrimination. They thought that it was neces-sary to maintain under altered conditions in war time the procedure laid down for such cases in time of peace. The object, to equip a battle-ship completely with the necessary provisions, etc., was not achieved.

My task was easier. I had to obtain beer, cigars and cigarettes for the wardroom. The fact that I still knew most of the people in the *Princess Alice* fairly well was a great help to me, and my raid was a success. Naturally I used the spare time in drinking good German beer in the mail steamer's mess—a rare enough treat for us in those days. My pleasure was detracted from by the thought that it would be a long time before it occurred again.

When everything was arranged, all the reserves who were also seamen were brought on board the *Emden*. Thus we gained Kapitänleutnant a. D. Klöpper and Vizesteuermann d. R. Meyer, two petty officers, two reserves, and six volun-teers. More men also volunteered, but we had to limit ourselves on account of lack of space.

At about seven o'clock we all returned to the *Emden*. Our guests from the island took a hearty leave of us, and went ashore in their own boat. The collier we had expected here never appeared, and we never discovered where she had gone astray. She remained lost.

The *Princess Alice* had been given orders to accompany us.

At about half-past seven we cast off from the *Markomannia* and put to sea on a south-westerly course with light war watches set. Our companions, the *Princess Alice* and the *Markomannia*, followed us right astern.

This position had, however, one disadvantage, in that the *Markomannia*, immediately following us, hid us from the *Princess Alice*. At first some evolutions had to be gone through, the orders for which were transmitted to our companions by lantern signals, and owing to this chance, in spite of slow speed, the *Princess Alice* once lost touch with us. In the *Emden* we were not aware of this, as all lights were, by order, completely hidden from sight. The impression given was that this ship desired to be independent, and the result was lack of co-ordination. There was a difficulty which also could not be avoided : the impossibility of giving the rendezvous by wireless. There were the strongest reasons why wireless should be used as little as possible. It was imperative that the enemy should not get to know the *Emden's* position.

It had now gone so far, however, that we were in serious need of the provisions in the *Princess Alice*, and it was therefore necessary to get into touch with her. This was accomplished by wireless in the night of August 20th, and a meeting-place was appointed for the next day. We received an answer, but it was very disappointing. The captain of the *Princess Alice* announced that he was short of coal, and the bad condition of his boilers, adding that the voyage and the meeting would have to be abandoned. He was then given orders to proceed, in order to avoid capture, into the neutral waters of the Philippines. We heard later that he had obeyed this order and reached his goal successfully. The behaviour of this captain was very peculiar, and our disappointment—one might even say anger—was comprehensible, for both the *Emden* and the *Markomannia* needed provisions. What that meant we were to learn : for two months we lived on corned beef and rice with a few dried vegetables, a maddening monotony. The officers' cook, Schultz, was a master in making up the stuff in a variety of different ways, but corned beef and rice remained what they were, and at last they are bound to become wearisome. As regards the men's food, it was our first consideration to procure the best for them, and to obtain fresh meat at every opportunity, e.g. from the supplies of the ships we captured later. The respect and preference given to the men in the question of food is, of course, natural, as they have more manual work to do than the officers, and therefore in greater need of and better claim to good nourishment. Adherence to this principle of care for the men's food was richly rewarded by the fact that we had few cases of illness during our cruise. That one man or another was occasionally affected by the very strenuous work could hardly be put down as illness.

After taking leave of the *Princess Alice* it was our first endeavour to get news of the attitude of Japan through to the cruiser squadron. The attempt to get into touch by wireless, naturally undertaken with all care, was unanswered. Our call was answered, however, to our great astonishment by the old light-cruiser *Geier*, formerly stationed in the South Seas, and she gave her position, so that the *Emden* was able to lay a course to meet her. Our Captain wished to talk to the captain of the *Geier*, Korvettenkapitän Grasshof, and a meeting was expected on August 21st.

It may have been three or four o'clock on that day when the look-out in the crow's nest sighted the *Geier*. At first a steamship very high out of the water came into sight, and a little later the *Geier*. It made a somewhat comic picture, as the light-cruiser was almost invisible beneath the height of the collier *Bochum*.

It was not long before we were so near that we could stop our engines, and the *Geier* put out a boat in which Korvettenkapitän Grasshof and his Adjutant, Oberleutnant zur See Sauerbeck, came on board the *Emden*. I was on watch at the time, and had therefore the task of getting everything clear for the reception of the visitors. Our Captain received them at the " Jacob's Ladder " (the boom had been stowed under the armoured deck for fear of splinters), and went into the cabin with them, where the situation was discussed and the *Geier* received instructions.

Not much could be done with the old light-cruiser. Her guns were light, her torpedo equipment obsolete, and her speed so low that in no case could she achieve more than twelve knots. She was so out-of-date that she must undoubtedly have fallen a prey to any modern hostile cruiser, and if she wished to carry on the war on merchant shipping they could most of them out-distance her. It was difficult for her captain to come to any decision.

If the *Princess Alice's* boilers had not been in such a bad condition it would have been possible to equip this altogether faster ship for use as an auxiliary cruiser.

According to reports which the *Emden* received later the *Geier*, however, met with some success, but was then obliged, as her boilers and engines had become quite untrustworthy, to put into Honolulu.

In less than an hour the *Geier's* two officers left the ship. Three hearty cheers were given on either side, and we carried on. The *Geier* disappeared in a north-easterly direction and we laid our course for the Straits of Molucca.

About that time we held several big fighting practices, so that all branches in the ship should be accustomed to working together.

On the evening of August 22nd we crossed the Equator, the first time I had done so. As we were at war, however, none of the usual " baptism " ceremonies were carried out. Magnificent weather and a sea like a mirror made this day more than usually beautiful.

On August 23rd we met with a Japanese passenger ship and with it an unpleasant situation, for although we knew of the dispatch of the Japanese ultimatum to Germany we did not know whether Japan had declared war. The Captain could not therefore take the decision to sink the vessel, and we suffered considerable chagrin at being forced to forgo this very choice morsel. The Japanese was very polite and hoisted and dipped her flag to us. She probably took us for an Englishman, as she could hardly have expected to find a German warship in these waters.

This day we saw a marvellous natural spectacle. Towards midday we met a school of porpoises, i.e. jumping fish, which heave themselves partly out of the water, and then, in spite of their numbers,

"EMDEN" WRECK, VIEW LOOKING FORWARD

reckoned almost by thousands, cleave the sea in
an ordered line as if they were on parade. For
over a quarter of an hour we had the pleasure of
watching the march-past of these ornamental
fish.

By the beginning of twilight we had reached
the end of the Straits of Molucca, and sighted
two lights, which we avoided in order that our
position should not become known. Probably
they were Dutch coast steamers whom we had
no wish to see. The end of the Straits of Molucca
is formed by the Amboina Channel and the islands
of Bouro and Ceram. There are also a number
of small islands of no importance, but useful to
sailors for purposes of navigation. We traversed
the Channel in darkness as we did not wish to be
sighted from the land.

We then laid our course for the Nusa-berei
Straits, which lie between the north-east point
of the island of Timor and the little island of
Letti, and are bounded on the east by some
small islands. A ship—if I am not mistaken it
was the *Tannenfeld*—had been ordered there to
provide us with coal. The reserves in the *Markomannia* were to be used as little as possible in
view of emergencies.

On August 24th we made towards the east
point of the island of Timor, a day before the
appointed meeting with the collier, and the
coaling, was to take place. In view of the hot
climate and heavy work for the men, this was

to commence before daybreak, and all the prepara
tions for coaling had been already made. The
organisers placed great reliance on the fact that
it would be possible to finish most of the work
during the early hours of the day, when it would
still be cool. It was of course also cool in the
evening, but then the men were tired and the
effort severe. We can look back with the greatest
thankfulness on the conduct of our splendid men
during hours that were very hard for them.

The *Emden* and *Markomannia* ran into the
meeting-place in the grey of morning on August
25th. The absentee was, of course, the collier.
Our ship was almost bare of coal, and had to be
coaled under any circumstances, so that the only
way was to relieve our companion, the *Markomannia*, of some of hers. It was not pleasant,
but our need was pressing.

We took in, by hard work, 470 tons from our
companion, so that the *Emden* had now once
more 950 tons on board. The Divisionsleutnants,
Leutnant z. S. Schall and I, joined in this work
by way of encouragement and example, and also
Leutnants z. S. Gyssling and Schmidt. As the
divisions were divided into starboard and port
watches, it became a point of honour with the
watches to come first, if possible, in the amount
got in, and I promised my men of the port watch
cigars as rewards if they should be first. It was
a joy to see them work, and I was glad to have
the opportunity of fulfilling my promise.

During the coaling a few men were sent ashore to look for fresh food for the live cow kept on board the *Markomannia*. I cannot remember if they had any success in their quest, but I know that there was great need of a run ashore for the men, while we were condemned to an atmosphere of coal dust.

CHAPTER IV

AFTER the coaling, during which the expected collier did not turn up, we put to sea again on a westerly course along the coast of Timor. Along with our other duties the ship had to be cleaned of the worst of her grime.

Our next goal was the island of Tanah Jampeia, where a ship had already been ordered to meet us. In the *Emden* we were all very pessimistic about the chances of her appearing.

The voyage itself, favoured by magnificent weather, was beautiful, being in continual view of land in the shape of small volcanic islands. On the port side we had the considerable height of the island of Timor, of over eight thousand feet.

During the night the wireless communications around us became much more lively and by intercepting many messages we got news that Brussels and Namur had fallen before the German attack. Naturally there was great rejoicing in the *Emden*.

On the morning of August 27th we came in sight of the island of Tanah Jampeia, and steered round it so as to enter the bay from the south.

Naturally nothing was to be seen of the expected steamship, but on the contrary a warship approached us flying her mast-head flags, and for a moment we were in doubt as to whether she was a Dutchman or an enemy. The order was given to clear ship for action, and the *Emden* also set her mast-head flags. The distance was about a mile and a half. Avoidance was not to be thought of, and firing could have been begun. At the last moment our Captain was able to make out that the stranger was flying the Dutch flag ; but there was nothing in her build to show her nationality, as she was coming directly head-on towards us. We at once lowered our flags.

The *Emden* pursued her course into the bay, and the Dutch battleship, the *Tromp*, crossed our bows and turned to follow us in. We now saw for the first time that there was a collier lying in the bay. Our joy was short-lived, however, for we soon saw that she was not German, but a Dutch ship, by name *Batavia*, and our spirits fell correspondingly.

That no formality should be lacking, our steam pinnace was called away in all haste to take an officer with the *Emden's* compliments to the *Tromp*, but the Dutchman was before us. A Dutch officer was already on his way to us and was soon on board the *Emden*. He was requested by the Captain to announce that Kapitän v. Müller himself would at once visit the *Tromp*.

By that time our pinnace was alongside and Kapitän v. Müller went across in her to the Dutchman.

Everyone in the *Emden* knew that this was a mere act of politeness to a neutral, but there was nevertheless some suspense, or rather a feeling as if some new turn of affairs was to be expected.

True enough, when our Captain returned we heard that the German collier which had been ordered there had called, but had been sent away by the Dutchman as the establishment of a German coaling point could not be permitted in Dutch waters. The Dutch captain had received instructions from his government to preserve the strictest neutrality. In addition it had been decided that warships of the states at war were only to be allowed to remain twenty-four hours in Dutch waters once in three months.

The Dutchman had therefore acted quite correctly, but our anxieties about coal were hardly reduced by his correctness. This captain was also pro-German in sympathy, and invited all the German officers on board his ship for a glass of beer.

Naturally this invitation was politely declined, as according to German ideas it would be a disgraceful thing to have all the officers out of the ship in war-time.

Emden and *Markomannia* weighed anchor and proceeded northwards, and the *Tromp* politely bore us company as far as the so-called **three**-mile limit. When we were out of neutral waters the Dutchman left us after the exchange of friendly signals.

We were scarcely out of sight when we laid our course for our actual objective, the Lombock Straits, which lay to the south.

In these days our fourth funnel made its appearance—not so beautiful as its brothers, but good enough to deceive from a distance. The originator of this idea was the first officer, Kapitänleutnant von Mücke. At first this structure was made of deck cloths, broad strips of stout sail cloth, with wooden frames at top and bottom, and the whole hoisted forward of our foremost funnel. Later we converted it to an oval shape, and added internal stiffening. From a distance we looked sufficiently like the English cruiser *Yarmouth* which was then on the East Asiatic station. I am convinced that many spies were deceived by this device.

From the point of view of our safety this idea must be acknowledged as brilliant. We wished to pass the Lombock Straits on August 28th on our way to the Indian Ocean, and there was a possibility that these quite narrow straits would be guarded by enemy torpedo boats or even cruisers. We were confirmed in this assumption by the liveliness of the wireless communication going on, and a Dutch message announced that a " torpedo boat with four funnels " had been sighted in the neighbourhood of Batavia.

We had therefore to be ready for anything and to take all care to be as little observed by the enemy as possible, as the Indian Ocean should be our best hunting ground.

Towards noon the mountains of the islands of Lombock and Bali came in sight on the east and west sides of the Lombock Straits.

Sunset was a magnificent sight. The dark rim of the mountains against a red-gold sky, all reflected in the sea, was worthy of the brush of a master.

As always in the tropics night fell quickly. Our fourth funnel, the false one, was hoisted, and sharp war watches were set and several special look-outs.

After a short time we sighted some sailing-ships. The passage proper began at about ten o'clock and many eyes strained into the night. We met one steamship and several sailing-ships, but no hostile warship was sighted. In the bright moonlight nothing was or could be missed. Shortly after midnight we were safely through, and a weight of care must have fallen from the heart of our Captain at reaching the objective without accident. We had made our approach completely unnoticed by the enemy.

For the next few days we steamed along the coasts of Sumatra and Java at about seventy sea miles distance, and in such beautiful weather the voyage afforded us much pleasure and a much-needed rest.

On August 30th, my birthday, in the morning,
I was awakened by a cheerful serenade by the
ship's orchestra. Since the outbreak of war, to
relieve the over-worked Adjutant, I had taken
over the work of band officer. My duties and
those of the band were not heavy—war gives
little opportunity for music—but still, on coaling
days the band always played to encourage the
men at their work, and their spirits were kept up
by it. I had in Wecke, the Uberhoboistenmaat,
an assistant to whom everything could as a rule
be left.

Our next objective was the island of Simalur,
to the north-westward of Sumatra, and the last
of the islands protecting it. Our captain had
selected it as suitable for coaling on account of
its sheltered bay, in which nothing could be seen
from the sea.

The voyage to this " homelike " island was of
some days length, and was occupied in shooting
practices and in cleaning the ship and, as far as
possible, the ship's sides as well.

The *Emden* at this time, to look at, bore little
resemblance to her pre-war nickname, " Swan of
the East." After so many coalings, in which her
sides had been ripped and struck and her paint
scratched and blackened, it was impossible for
her to remain white as a swan, and the sea-water
had had the further effect that she had slowly
but surely become rusty. Naturally painting was
done where possible, in patches and stripes, but

there was no time to go over her thoroughly.
Dust and blackness exuded continually from the
deck stores, for we had sacks of coal piled on our
deck. Usually, of course, coal was carried in the
bunkers, but for the long voyages we had to make
in war time an extra supply was necessary, which
was stored on deck in sacks, on the quarterdeck
and the after-part of the forecastle. We thus
carried larger stores of coal and at the same time
spared the men—though not the linoleum on the
decks. To keep this clean and good, especially on
the quarterdeck, was to some extent a regulation
which was faithfully carried out, but the frequent
coaling certainly scratched and tore it, and towards
the end of the cruise it was completely destroyed
by the rough handling it had to undergo under
the circumstances. War was war, and the *Emden*
a warship, and not engaged on a pleasure trip.
The main consideration was the fighting trim of
the *Emden*, and a good state of health on board.
The men had to be kept healthy and cheerful.
In general this was achieved, but there were some
things which seemed to warrant anxiety, principally in the matter of nourishment. Everything
was arranged so that the men should be provided
with fresh food for as long a time as possible.
The officers willingly stood aside in favour of the
men, and the wardroom had already for some
time had no fresh provisions while the men were
still getting them. The peace-time stock of tinned
provisions was plentiful, and when the fresh food

for the wardroom was finished there were plenty
of "tinned titbits"; but *paté de foie gras*, for
instance, when constantly repeated as a principal
article of diet, awakens a most remarkable hunger
for ordinary fresh meat.

Our Captain concerned himself in a touching
and fatherly way to procure for the men as much
fresh food as possible, and saw personally to the
proper distribution of it; for Kapitän z. S. von
Müller was one of the gallant type of man who
does everything for others and remains himself
obscurely in the background.

This truly noble man died on March 11th, 1923,
in Braunschweig, of inflammation of the lungs.
All who knew him mourned him from their hearts.
In his greatness of character and goodness of
heart he was a friendly captain, always ready
with help, and, to those who had the privilege of
knowing him more closely, an excellent, constant
and steadfast friend. In the *Emden*, I, as a mere
Lieutenant, had no proper opportunity to come
into closer relations with Kapitän von Müller, and
only after November 11th, 1914, did I come into
prolonged and active contact with him. For so
long as he was with us in captivity at Malta he
was in the truest sense a good counsellor to me,
and I may also say a faithful comrade.

To return now to the year 1914, on August 13th
we first intercepted a wireless message in cipher
from a warship which gave the identification
signal Q.M.D., which was much debated in the

Emden. We thought at first of the English armoured-cruiser *Minotaur*, but later came to the conclusion that it was the *Hampshire,* which was later confirmed after we were taken prisoners.

The Dutch and Siamese wireless stations gave every evening the latest news from the theatres of war, which caused great rejoicing in the *Emden* by their reports of German successes. The news that the French Government had been frightened out of Paris to Bordeaux was received with special acclamation.

There were beaming faces on board and the ship's company went about their daily duties with redoubled zeal and rejoicing.

On September 3rd we came in sight of a group of islands, among which was Simalur, with its snug harbour. As the *Emden* did not wish to arrive there till next morning, speed was accordingly reduced.

The bay which we intended to enter bore the name of Langini Harbour, although the expression " harbour " did not quite correspond with the reality. It consisted of an oval bay with a very narrow entrance protected by several small islands. The " port " of this " harbour " consisted of a few native huts.

The place was simply a sanctuary, a place in which to coal free from observation, and a better could not be desired.

We passed by the island in the darkness and

saw the blink of lights in the harbour town to the south of us. On this night the wireless sent out by the English warship using the cipher Q.M.D. was particularly frequent and loud, from which we inferred that she must be somewhere in the vicinity.

We later found out that this ship was then patrolling the vicinity daily in search of German warships, and was anchored that evening off the south-west point of the island of Simalur. If, therefore, we had appeared there early in the morning, we must have run into the arms of the *Hampshire*, which would probably have cost the *Emden* dear. Some good angel, however, prevented this.

On September 4th, at six o'clock in the morning, we ran into the quiet bay. It looked heavenly. The narrow entrance thickly framed in mangroves, and behind them the primeval forest in all the magnificence of the tropics, was the most superb sight I have ever seen. New and beautiful pictures greeted our delighted eyes as we passed further in, and after a long sea voyage the impression was unforgettable.

A fairy land indeed, but the collier we expected was not there, and our companion, the *Markomannia*, had to help us out again. There was a buoy to mark the place where she should anchor, and when she was anchored the *Emden* went alongside her and made fast.

As a precaution a lieutenant and a signalman

were posted in the foremost crow's nest to keep a look out for any enemy vessel. On the other hand, it was harder for the enemy to discover us.

Coaling began at nine o'clock, and enough had to be got in to bring the *Emden's* supplies up to 1,000 tons.

Had it been cool weather the men would have been able to accomplish this task. In the warm, damp temperature of the tropics, however, which was particularly noticeable here, it was impossible although they worked willingly. The men and the officers, who also joined in and helped, were exhausted before midday. Nevertheless, coaling was continued after the meal up to eleven o'clock that night, and 450 tons were brought on board. The idea of working all night could not be carried out as with all good will the men could do no more. We therefore turned in so as to take up work fresh in the morning. All possible consideration for the men was observed in watch-keeping that night, and only light watches were set, consisting of one Oberleutnant and the indispensable posts. All the rest enjoyed a much-needed rest.

Since the outbreak of war Schall and I had had our night quarters in the wardroom as our cabin was on the lower deck and somewhat inaccessible in case of any alarm. I slept in a hammock and Schall slept beneath me on a mattress.

Thus we slept after the strenuous day in Langini Bay. Our sleep had been well earned, and was deep and quiet, but it did not last long. At about three o'clock in the morning we were awakened by a piercing " miaouw," the complaint of a cat which is " not quite well." The noise was fearful, and my wrath great over the unnecessary disturbance. I cursed most heartily, but the miaouwing was not affected. The beast cared not a button for the wrath of a Leutnant zur See, worn-out with coaling and only anxious to sleep.

What was really the matter with the confounded cat I could not at first discover. Such a clamour could not be caused by sea-sickness. It must be some bodily illness. Only one thing was clear to me, that it must be our own cat, for no other cat could by any possibility have smuggled itself on board the *Emden*. These considerations, however, did not put an end to the noise. On the contrary, the miaouwing became stronger, and was mingled with another noise which often resembled a child's crying. With the honourable intention of dissuading pussy from her evening song, I extracted a box of matches from my trouser pocket and tried to produce enough light to light up the scene and the " singing " cat. To be sure, pussy's behaviour annoyed me, but what disturbed me even more was the fact that comrade Schall ignored the cat's concert and went on sleeping quietly. Scarcely had I lighted the match, however, when my rage was changed into convulsions of laughter. In the madness of

my mirth I broke the peace of the night more
effectively than any feline creature which had
just presented a fourth kitten to the Sumatran
world—between the legs of the sleeping Leutnant
z. S. Schall.

Four healthy kittens lay curled up with their
mother in the welcome warmth radiating from
comrade Schall. Distinctly a novelty in the
annals of the *Emden*, and highly entertaining.
A delightful family picture !

What my curses had not effected my laughter
did. Leutnant z. S. Schall rubbed his eyes and
discovered by the feeble light of my match the
comic surprise-packet between his legs, the five
cats of the *Emden*.

A lieutenant with an utterly confounded expression and a comrade in tears with laughter !
Schall did not know whether to laugh or curse
at such disrespectful behaviour. One eye laughed
and the other scattered sparks about the bulkheads—an unforgettable comedy.

The mother-cat and her offspring were removed
Schall turned his mattress and went off to sleep
again. The cats were taken care of by members
of the crew, and the little ones later disappeared,
where to I know not.

In the early morning at six coaling began
again. At all costs it had to be hurried, for the
Emden had to get her full supply of coal on board
as quickly as possible and be able to vanish with
the *Markomannia* before the Dutch discovered

them. The reason was the regulation of the
Dutch Government, that warships of the bel-
ligerents could only remain in Dutch waters
for twenty-four hours in three months. If we
could get away from Simalur without being seen
it would be all in our favour, for we should still
have our twenty-four hours unexpended.

At eight in the morning, however, the *Emden's*
lookout announced that a small white steam-
yacht flying the Dutch flag was approaching the
bay. We were caught.

Soon after the Government boat ran in and
anchored right beside us. The Government officer
lost no time in coming across to us, and we all
knew the reason. We were to disappear, as our
twenty-four hours was already up, and we should
have to leave neutral waters. In the presence
of the insistent Dutchman, Kapitän von Müller
asked the engineer of the *Emden*, Marine-Oberingenieur Ellerbroek, when the engines of the
two ships would be ready for sea.

Ellerbroek caught the deeper meaning in this
remark and replied that at least two more hours
would be required.

The Dutchman granted us the two hours, and
accepted for himself whisky and iced soda-water
to quiet his conscience completely.

Our men needed no explanation of the urgency
of the situation. They guessed it all, fell to with
threefold energy, and by eleven o'clock the *Emden*
had completed her 1,000 tons. In the infernal

Oriental heat these men worked wonders on behalf of their country.

At the sound of the order to cast off from the now lightened *Markomannia*, the Dutchman took his leave, cooler both in body and spirit, and the two ships immediately took their way out of the ideal harbour of Simalur.

For some time after we were out of the threatening eyes of the Dutchman we kept to a south-easterly course. Afterwards, however, we steamed northwards, making for our real objective, the steamship route from Khota Raja to Colombo.

The weather, which had hitherto been beautiful, now deteriorated, turning to very strong white squalls, which were welcome to us, although troublesome, for our fresh water had now got very low. We replenished our stores by spreading out all our vessels, which were filled by the kindness of the heavens.

What we lacked even more than water was soap, the index of civilisation, as some uncharitable people have said who have never had to endure its lack in a ship. It had become a luxury for us, with which it was necessary to be extremely sparing, to such an extent that the water in which the men washed was saved to wash first their clothes and then the decks.

The squalls brought a sea with them, and the *Emden* was now dipping her bows deep and fairly frequently. Our first objective, the aforementioned steamship route, was reached on September 7th, and the purpose of the cruise was begun, namely, not to miss a single ship using the route. Eyes and glasses were continually in use, as everyone wished to be the first to be able to report smoke in sight.

Like the hunter, a sailor also needs a little luck, for which we in the *Emden* hoped in vain. Our many hours of cruising brought us nothing. We would have to search elsewhere, and so altered course and made for the steamer line from Negabatang to Khota Raja on our way to the line between Colombo and Rangoon.

We reached it on September 8th, but again several hours of cruising brought no result, except the conviction that the capturing of enemy merchant ships was not so easy as had been supposed at first. We began to learn modesty, and withdrew some of our expectations. There was no witchcraft in it, but simply the fact that on the three lines we had searched there was not one ship to be found, not even a sailing vessel.

The huntsman's patience is also needed by the seaman, and we altered course again towards the important line from Colombo to Calcutta.

Fortune was still against us, but she winked, for we had scarcely reached the line at eleven o'clock at night in the friendly darkness when the look out reported " A light four points on the starboard bow."

Sighs of relief were heard. The order " Clear

ship for Action" rang through the ship like a release.

We were after her full speed, the *Markomannia* following faithfully as best she could.

Courage, suspense, and rejoicing were mixed within us, with some anger at the delay that was necessary before we could make out what sort of a ship we had found. Soon we could at least make out that she was a merchantman.

Two rounds of blank were fired to stop her, and the Morse lamp spelt out the message in English : "Stop your engines. Don't use the wireless."

The stranger obeyed at once.

The prize crew had been told off beforehand, and was commanded by Oberleutnant z. S. d. R. Lauterbach. Armed to the teeth they were rowed over and went on board the stranger. Things passed slowly for the curiosity on board the *Emden*, for although the stranger was lighted up by the searchlights it was impossible to make out her nationality, and we were, of course, anxious to know both this and the nature of her cargo, which Lauterbach was to find out and communicate to us by signal.

At last the Morse lamp blinked out the message : " Greek steamship, *Pontoporos* ! "

There was weeping and gnashing of teeth that we should have lighted on a neutral for our first prize. Naturally she must be allowed to go on her way.

But Lauterbach had not finished : " Carrying 6,500 tons of coal for English Government. Is on her way from Calcutta to Bombay."

She was carrying contraband, which could be confiscated, and coal at that, which the *Emden* could use so well. For us in time of war it was worth more than diamonds and pearls.

The Greek and the *Emden* exchanged chagrin with rejoicing.

What was dictated by the necessity of war was at once carried out, and the prize crew was enlarged by a number of engine-room ratings from the *Emden*, while those who were now not needed in the *Pontoporos* returned to us. Lauterbach was now put in command of the Greek.

The Captain of the *Emden* asked the Greek captain if he would be willing, on receipt of proper payment, to do service to Germany as represented by the *Emden*.

The answer, received by Morse, was to the effect that both he and his command would readily do so. It was the same to him whether he served England or Germany. The main point was the payment.

The Greek's consent simplified matters very much, as the coal could not be taken in at once. It was troublesome, however, that he could only steam at nine knots, which hampered the *Emden* considerably.

Lauterbach signalled that everything was in

order in the *Pontoporos*, and we proceeded onwards in company. In order to have them in
sight the *Markomannia* was stationed to starboard
and the *Pontoporos* to port.

Naturally we kept to our former course on the
Colombo-Calcutta route and kept even more
strict lookout.

At eight in the morning on September 10th a
smoke cloud was sighted to the north. The
Emden flew towards it, leaping and cutting through
the water.

As the *Emden* came nearer we could make out
a large steamship with a very unusual super-
structure. It was an Englishman with the blue
ensign waving proudly at her stern. The question
was whether she had been chartered by the
Admiralty or was being run by the British Government.

She had no suspicions and steamed peacefully
towards us, probably in the belief that the *Emden*
was an English warship. Otherwise her unwary
conduct was incomprehensible.

She was carefully studied from the *Emden* and
we came to the conclusion that she was not armed.
We therefore fired one warning round, hoisted
the German ensign and at the same time the
international signal " Stop ! do not use wireless."

The Englishman harkened to necessity and
stopped, and a search and prize crew was sent
over under Oberleutnant z. S. v. Levetzow and
Vizesteuermann d. R. Meyer.

She was captured in 84° 2′ E. and 10° 48′ N.

Levtezow inspected her papers and signalled : "Steamship *Indus*, 3,413 tons, en route from Calcutta to Bombay for the Indian government. Is equipped to carry troops and horses, which she is to take to Europe."

Not bad ! The *Emden* had just caught the fellow in time, before bringing Indian troops to Europe to fight against Germany. It was a pity that the soldiers were not already in her as then she would have been even more welcome.

As a trooper the *Indus* had been provided by the practical English with ample stores of provisions, a fact which gave us considerable satisfaction. What pleased us most, however, was that she was carrying an almost fantastic amount of soap. The reader may be surprised at such rejoicing over soap at sea in war time, but seafolk like cleanliness and everyone was delighted at the news.

We thanked the English government in our thoughts for their far-reaching consideration and their care to supply us with all we had been wanting.

Our second cutter was at once called away to make the necessary removals from the *Indus*.

There were a good many arrangements to make as a result of this capture. For instance the necessary exchanges had to be made in both our companion ships the *Markomannia* and the *Pontoporos*. As the *Markomannia* was to take

over the crew of the *Indus*, Kapitänleutnant
d. R. Klöpper was made military commandant
on board the *Indus*. The *Pontoporos* received
the first officer of the *Markomannia* as captain
and the latter was given Vizesteurmann d. R.
Meyer as military officer. Corresponding watches
were established on both ships.

When these arrangements had been completed
we joined forces for the transfer of the article we
were so much in need of, and of provisions. Soap
first, of course, laid up in mountains in the *Emden*,
and then fresh provisions. Finally we took over
the tools and instruments of navigation, of which
there can never be enough. As the men, however,
were not quite familiar with the idea of what
was or was not necessary, at about noon our
first officer went across to the *Indus* to supervise
the matter personally. The Captain had tried to
hasten the transfer as much as possible, but a
decision was hard to make, and faced with the
treasures with which the *Indus* was filled even
the heart of a first officer could not remain quite
hard.

It was four o'clock in the afternoon before our
needs were satisfied. Kapitän von Müller, as
ever, knew exactly what he wanted, and declared
the matter at an end.

Our upper deck looked like a colossal warehouse. There were stocks, or at least samples
of everything. There were towels, soap, linen,
tinned foods, fresh meat, live hens and ducks,

drinks, nautical instruments, charts, pencils, and some very welcome oilskins with which we could re-equip the cutters' crews and the watches against bad weather.

Finally the ship had to be sunk. The burial of a ship in the open sea! For this purpose a sinking party went on board the *Indus* consisting of one engineer, a petty officer, and three stokers. They removed the doors between the boiler rooms and the engine room. The sea-cocks were then opened, so that the water could pass freely into the lower compartments of the ship. When this had been done the sinking party returned to the *Emden*.

The gunnery section was then ordered to begin their activities by firing a few shells to help the *Indus* under, but for the present the *Indus* did not seem inclined to sink. Too much ammunition could not be wasted, and the ship was bound to sink after the sea-cocks had been opened. It was an hour, however, before she began to sink, and then slowly, though surely. She slanted to one side, and shipped a good deal of water. Then the bows sank, and all at once she sank gurgling into the depths—an uncanny spectacle.

The escaping air made a loud report and scattered a mass of things in the air, the masts sprang several yards out of the water and fell back on to the flat surface with loud reports.

Some of the *Indus's* boats were also left floating, and could neither be taken in nor easily destroyed.

This was unpleasant for us, as they might betray, perhaps to the enemy, that the *Emden* had been in these waters, carrying on the war on merchant shipping. But we could lose no more time over them as there were more important things to be done. We therefore proceeded on a northerly course, *Emden* ahead, *Markomannia* following.

It was decided not to leave the fruitful steamship routes, but to capture other ships, until the disappearance of the ships that had been announced aroused the enemy and lead to a search for the cause. According to our instructions we meant to use every opportunity to damage the enemy. War is war!

The night passed quietly, nothing being sighted. The morning of September 11th was devoted to the division of the spoils. Kapitänleutnant von Mücke sat like a Pasha on his treasures, and allotted them to the various divisions. During this process the unnecessary articles came to light which had been brought over in yesterday's hurry, and they were now thrown summarily over the side as there was no object in increasing our ballast with unnecessary lumber.

We officers had scarcely finished our simple lunch when we felt the *Emden* turn and increase speed. What now?

We all tumbled curiously up on deck to see what was happening, and at once discovered that another ship was in sight.

At hunting speed we soon came up with our prey, and signalled : " Stop, etc. . . ."

The enemy heard at once, and stopped, and Lauterbach, as the most experienced prize officer of the *Emden*, was sent over with the necessary party.

An Englishman again, the *Lovat*, 6,012 tons, equipped as a trooper, and chartered by the Indian government. Her destination was Bombay, and she was captured in 86° 32′ E., 16° 25′ N. There was now no scarcity in the *Emden*, and we had no intention of wanton robbery. What our Captain wanted from this prize was only newspapers, and news. Lauterbach was given strict orders to confiscate all newspapers in the *Lovat* and bring them back with him.

The crew of the *Lovat*, the latter being destined for destruction, were, as is customary, given a period in which to pack up their possessions and make ready to leave the ship for ever. They were all brought aboard the *Markomannia*, where the imprisoned captain of the *Indus* was rubbing his hands over the fate of his comrades in the *Lovat* and preparing to greet his fellow-sufferers.

The *Lovat* was to be destroyed like the *Indus*, but with all her cargo, by boring bulkheads, opening the sea-cocks, and a few shells. She was, however, as obstinate as the *Indus* and did not want to sink although she had to. As darkness fell before she did so, we left the spot and abandoned her to her inevitable fate.

The papers brought by Lauterbach were examined and thoroughly laughed over, being full of stories which a baby would scarcely have taken for good coin. Lately we had been kept up to date by the neutral wireless stations about the events in the theatres of war, and we were astonished at the lies which the English papers dished out to the Indians. It was, of course, understandable from the English point of view, for the Indian natives, who had not too much enthusiasm for the British oppressor, had to be won over or at least hindered from rioting.

Much more interesting for us was the news from the *Markomannia*, where the interned captains had meanwhile been livened up by whisky and soda and had disclosed in their chatter some very important news for the *Emden*. This was accordingly signalled across to us. The purport was that behind them were three more ships equipped as troopers which had already left Calcutta.

This was very pleasant for the *Emden*, saving her further search. She could wait quietly while one Englishman after another ran into her arms and was sunk. We therefore steamed slowly along the steamer line on a course for Calcutta, keeping our eyes open.

Towards ten o'clock in the evening a light was reported ahead. Number one of the expected ships ! She was coming directly towards the *Emden*, so that we hardly needed to increase speed. This time the customary signal was not accompanied by a gun, the siren being enough. The usual signal to stop was given, and the order to use no wireless.

The stranger obeyed.

As it was intended to subject this ship to a closer search next morning, a prize crew was sent aboard in the meantime, under Lauterbach and Leutnant z. S. Gyssling, who had orders to keep by the *Emden*. This time the signal ran : " English ship *Kabinga*, 4,657 tons, with cargo of piece goods. From Calcutta to Bombay, Port Said, Mediterranean and New York." She had a speed of 10 knots. Her cargo was valuable, but of little use to us, as the majority was American property. According to international law we could have sunk her, but we would have been bound to pay for the neutral cargo. This did not please Kapitän von Müller, and he decided to use this ship as a depository for the crews of the ships we had sunk and leave her in the next harbour. Without this resource it would have become necessary in time to use one of the captured ships for this purpose, and this Englishman with a neutral cargo seemed to be specially designed for the need. In addition to this the English captain had his wife and children with him on board—not of course a decisive factor, but one which offered the opportunity of showing

our consideration for them, and how Germany
conducted her war on merchant shipping.

The matters of command and setting up guards
in the *Kabinga* were therefore settled, and the
Emden, followed by her train, proceeded on her
way.

All the officers of the *Emden* who were not on
duty turned in after the recent strain, and they
all were glad of the night's rest.

We did not sleep long, for only about three
hours later the order was given : " Clear ship for
Action."

The devil ! What was in it this time ?

Seizing the necessary clothing we rushed to
our action stations, and I accordingly to my
pacing of the torpedo flat. This position had
the disadvantage that one could not satisfy one's
curiosity, as there below we could see nothing,
and could only gather indirectly from the conning
tower, with which we were connected by a speaking tube, what was happening above. By this
means the news reached me that there was no
question of a warship, but only a merchantman,
and there was therefore no torpedo work for me.
I therefore stationed myself beneath the bridge,
from which position everything could be seen
without getting in anybody's way. There was
too little room on the bridge itself, and one
would have been in the way of the Captain and
officer of the watch.

In the same way as the *Kabinga*, the new

steamer was stopped by siren and megaphone
(86° 24' E., 17° 55' N.). Oberleutnant z. S. Levetzow and Leutnant z. S. Zimmermann went on
board the ship with the search and prize party.

Soon afterwards came the message : " English
coaling-steamer *Killin*, with 6,000 tons of Indian
coal, from Calcutta to Bombay, speed eight to
nine knots."

In the meantime the *Markomannia*, *Pontoporos*,
and *Kabinga* had come up with us.

As the work of careful search and sinking had
to be undertaken by daylight our proud squadron
then proceeded on the previous course, with the
Emden ahead, *Kabinga* and *Markomannia* on the
starboard quarter and *Pontoporos* and *Killin* on
the port quarter.

We thus had a good view of our convoy, which
was necessary for the control of the darkening
arrangements. On a dark night a ship can be
betrayed at a great distance by a single light,
and this we naturally wished to avoid, lest our
fruitful activities should be prematurely cut short
by hostile warships. This of course had to be
reckoned with every hour. Our voyage was no
life insurance, as we were all aware, no less than
of the fact that the day must come when the
gallant *Emden* must make acquaintance with
the bottom of the sea. We had no liking for the
idea, but were resolved to sell our lives dearly.

On the morning of September 13th fine work
began for our cutters' crews who had to transfer

the English ships' companies to the *Kabinga*, which was now to act as a dump, by rowing them over from the *Markomannia*, where they had hitherto been confined. As the sea was high this work was very severe, in spite of the fact that the *Emden* gave them her lee to work under.

Lauterbach returned on board the *Emden*, and during the transfer Oberleutnant z. S. Geerdes took over his duties.

Meanwhile the sinking party had completed their unpleasant work on the *Killin*, and at about ten in the morning she was given a few German shells by way of leave taking, and thereupon plunged, bows first, for ever into the depths—not without the usual sprinkling of parts of the ship, which broke loose, sprang gracefully out of the water and fell back noisily. Of the *Killin* it was the funnel which aspired to heaven, but in the end was forced to sink again in the sea.

We had already practice in the sinking of enemy ships and looked upon it as part of our duties, and it was carried out adroitly and quickly.

We then continued our cruise in the direction of Calcutta with growing curiosity as to what our next surprise would be.

The afternoon was at first peaceful. We lieutenants who were not on duty were playing bridge and had just finished a rubber when someone came into the wardroom with the news that a smoke cloud was again in sight.

We threw in our cards, naturally, and went up on the quarterdeck to watch the smoke through our glasses.

The *Emden* approached the new victim at full speed. She was a good-sized ship with a big funnel, and presently we could make out that she was flying the English red ensign.

We were naturally pleased, as it would have been a pity if such a ship had been a neutral. She was captured 86° 24' E. and 18° 1' N.

When the Englishman had stopped, Lauterbach and his party went across and we received the message : " English steamship *Diplomat*, 7,615 tons, with ten thousand tons of tea, from Calcutta to England."

Our Captain at once decided that the ship was to be sunk on the spot, but this time directed by the first torpedo-officer, Oberleutnant z. S. Witthoeft. The necessary party, armed with blasting cartridges, were soon got together and sent aboard the *Diplomat*. The English ship's company left the ship, the cartridges were laid, sea-cocks opened, the cartridges were touched off all together, and the ship abandoned at once. The last man had scarcely left the ship when the explosion took place.

Meanwhile the *Emden* had sighted another smoke cloud, which was immediately pursued. It was a steamship, but the flag could not yet be identified. It was settled that Levetzow and I were to deal with her, but to our great disappointment we made out, on nearer approach, the commercial ensign of Italy. She was a neutral, and more than that, an ally, or rather one of the Triple Alliance.

We boarded the ship with mixed feelings and were received by the captain with some acidity. Levetzow asked for the ship's name and papers, received the necessary information, and signalled : " Italian steamer *Loredano, en route* to Calcutta." Kapitän von Müller sent back that the captain of the *Loredano* should be asked to take over the crews of the ships which had been captured and sunk, about two hundred men.

Meanwhile, I had set guards and taken a look into the hold. The ship did not seem to be fully laden. Except for a small cargo of crude wool there was nothing of importance in the *Loredano*.

Levetzow called me to him, as the captain understood no English whatever. I was to try to convey our Captain's wishes to him. Italian was no good, as I understood only a few phrases, but in French we had a little success. The Italian captain, however, did not wish to convey the men to Calcutta, not even for payment, and he remained stiff-neckedly obstinate after my explanation that sufficient provisions could be provided for them. We had hoped in this way to get rid of all the crews and to be able to sink the *Kabinga*.

Friendly words were useless. Our Italian " ally " remained acid, however hard I tried to

convince him. During these negotiations the
Diplomat, with an elegant swing, had softly taken
leave, and with diplomatic quietness gone to the
bottom.

Levetzow of course signalled the result of the
fruitless discussions to the *Emden.*

This refusal was annoying, and I tried my hand
again with the fellow, and hit upon a ruse. Word
by word I said to him in the French language :
" Captain, what would you do if the *Emden* were
to turn these crews adrift in boats ? "

He answered : " I should then, of course, be
forced to take them on board."

I therefore proceeded : " If you would do this,
there can be no objection to your taking them on
board at once, and you would gain by it as well,
for if you take them voluntarily you will receive
money and provisions for them."

Enlightenment began to dawn upon the Vene-
tian, and after some consideration he declared
himself agreeable.

Levetzow at once signalled this decision to our
Captain, but it was now dark and the transfer
of the men, always awkward, was not desirable
at night.

Kapitän von Müller sent back that the Italian's
help was not now desired. It had been decided
meanwhile to use the *Kabinga* as a dump after all.

There was therefore nothing left but to leave
the *Loredano,* but before this Levetzow demanded
the Italian's word of honour that he would

preserve strict neutrality and assist in no proceedings hostile to the *Emden*, which promise he gave.

Back in the *Emden* we were glad to have nothing more to do with this captain. The last two hours had been no pleasure to us.

The *Emden* and her train left this position about half-past seven.

The *Loredano* also steamed away in the direction of Calcutta, and as no one trusted him we at first kept a course to southwards, and only later returned to a northerly course. Common sense demanded that we should now leave the Colombo-Calcutta line.

CHAPTER V

OUR new objective was the steamer line
Madras-Calcutta, on which we hoped for
rich booty. At about ten o'clock in the
evening the lookout reported a light, and we
went after it cleared for action. We could soon
make out that it was a steamship, and signalled :
" Stop your engines, don't use wireless, what
ship ? "

In answer we received one word : " *Dandolo.*"
Another Italian !

We had no wish to be recognised and signalled
back : " Thank you, good voyage ! " And we
went on our way, keeping at first to a fictitious
course. Our discretion had the unwelcome result
that we lost our companion, who could not
follow so quickly.

In the search for our convoy we just missed
ramming the *Kabinga.* The situation was saved
by both ships going full speed astern. We then
fell in together and laid a course for the steamer
line Madras-Calcutta.

The night passed quietly and brought us
welcome rest and recovery from the strain of the
last few days.

On September 14th, in the morning, the pagoda

of Puri came in sight and we made for it, as at first sight it looked, owing to a mirage, like a ship. The mistake was only discovered when we were near it, which put us in a very unpleasant situation, as the strong landward current had brought us into a region with many shallows, and we were in danger of going on the mud, to escape which we had to retreat again.

When we were in clear water again we stopped to complete the transhipment of the English crews, which we had not been able to finish yesterday. To-day the *Kabinga* was to be abandoned with all the foreigners in her. The work was again carried out by the cutters. The prize crew of the *Kabinga* and the military commando from the *Markomannia*, under Kapitän-leutnant Klöpper, left her and returned on board.

Soon afterwards another ship with the British flag was sighted, which the *Emden* at once "adopted" (19° 55′ N., 87° 10′ E.). She was ordered to join our convoy, and did so. The prize crew, under Lauterbach and Leutnant z. S. Fikentscher, were sent across, and at the same time the sinking and blasting parties, under Oberleutnant z. S. v. Levetzow, went on board the new prize.

The ship was the *Trabbock*, 4,028 tons, a collier without a cargo, on her way from the Indian harbour of Negapatang to Calcutta. The English ship's company was quickly brought on board

The Buckled Deck of the "Emden"

the *Kabinga*, which was at once detached. The " dump " took leave politely, with three cheers for the *Emden*, and vanished into the darkness.

This unexpected ovation gave great pleasure in the *Emden*—a recognition of the considerate treatment we had willingly conceded as far as the circumstances would allow.

The *Trabbock* came to a rather different end from the other ships we had sunk, making quite a spectacle. As soon as the prize and blasting parties had left her there was a very powerful explosion, accompanied by tremendous flames. The coal-dust in her had been ignited, and the colossal flames made wonderful fireworks against the blackness of the night.

The *Emden* did not wait for the end, but proceeded on her previous course.

In half an hour a light was reported on the starboard beam, and the *Emden* was after it at full speed. The stranger must have been warned, however, or have seen the flames of the *Trabbock*, as she got up steam and went full speed to try to escape the *Emden*.

A chase ! A chase on the high seas and in darkness. The *Emden* was without question the faster ship and soon was within signalling distance of the quarry, to whom she gave the order to stop, by siren.

The stranger made further efforts to escape. A few rounds of blank backed up the order to stop, but the quarry left this summons also unheeded. The *Emden's* patience was exhausted and a shot was placed across her bows. At that she stopped. Position of capture, 19° 55′ N., 87° 11′ E. The *Emden* sent the question: 'What ship?'

The answer came obediently: "*Clan Matheson.*"

An English ship, and one that must have a guilty conscience concerning the value of her cargo, as she had tried to escape.

Lauterbach and Schall looked after the further investigations—4,775 tons, piece-goods cargo, from England to Calcutta: and a valuable cargo it was, consisting of motors, locomotives, bicycles, typewriters, and other fine things. The most valuable passenger was a race-horse, which we heard later had been already entered on the list of the Calcutta Racing Club.

The utmost speed was demanded for the dispatch of this Englishman. Klöpper and a party for military duties went over to the *Markomannia* again, and at the same time she took on board, in spite of the darkness, the English ship's company. The blasting and sinking parties were also working at full speed.

Within forty-five minutes everything had been done, and the English ship, complete with typewriters, race-horse, etc., was sunk.

The *Emden* took an easterly course. Our objective was Preparis North Channel. These straits are protected by the Andaman Islands, and seemed specially suitable for the coaling which had now become necessary. We had taken in nothing since September 5th.

We received that night a wireless message sent out by the Calcutta light-ship, which awakened no little anger in the *Emden*, and ran as follows : '' As reported by the Italian steamship *Loredano*, the German cruiser *Emden* has sunk the *Diplomat*, *Kabinga*, and *Pontoporos*, at 86° 24′ E., 18° 1′ N.''

An unpleasant business ! The Italian captain had not kept his word. A breach of faith and rank betrayal of an ally could not have been expected or foreseen. Also the news in the message was not correct, as the *Kabinga* and *Pontoporos* were not sunk. We heard later that this betrayal was rewarded by the Indian Government. The captain received a gold watch and chain—the reward of Judas.

The *Kabinga* also broadcasted as follows : '' The German cruiser *Emden*, with the collier *Markomannia*, has sunk outside Calcutta the steamships *Indus, Lovat, Killin, Diplomat and Trabbock*. The *Kabinga* herself was abandoned with all the ships' companies.''

September 15th was for us a day of complete rest. We were steaming on no steamer route, and a meeting was as good as impossible. Our gallant men had to be granted their rest, for the last few days had taxed their strength to the utmost.

We officers were also glad of the day of rest,

which we needed in order to be prepared for further efforts.

In the evening we received the news sent out by the Calcutta wireless station. It was all concerned with our doings, and ended with the advice : " Look out for the *Emden*."

In the Bay of Bengal, the part of the Indian Ocean where the *Emden* had done most harm to the enemy, our ship was sufficiently known. After coaling we would have to seek further fields and work to some extent more secretly.

September 16th brought brilliant weather and a sea like a mirror, and our Captain decided to use the day for coaling at sea. It was our first effort of this kind. This time the *Pontoporos* was to be made use of, and her coal transferred to the *Emden*. We therefore went alongside her and made fast, using improvised fenders (known as " baskets " and " elephants' eyes ") and wash-boards placed between the two ships, so that our freeboard should not be too much damaged by the shifting and coming together of the ships. The *Pontoporos* lay on our starboard side.

After the *Emden* had made fast sufficiently she went dead slow ahead with her starboard engines, while the *Pontoporos* kept her engines stopped. The coaling began at about nine o'clock, and at first the two after-holds were broached. On account of the great heat the work was again not easy, but what made it almost unbearable was the quality of the coal, which was slack and dust.

The coal we had taken from the *Markomannia* had been Shantung coal, and consisted of large solid pieces, which were both easy to work with and gave good fuel value. Difficulties soon began with the unloading of the *Pontoporos'* coal. We succeeded in boring a hole in a heap of coal, so as to get at it from two sides, but the two sides immediately fell together again, and the work had to be begun again. One could not blame the men for the oaths used, and we officers who worked with them were in the fullest sympathy with their cursing, for the distasteful work and the choking dust was no better for us.

Discretion made it necessary to hurry, and towards midday some Indian coolies, who had belonged to the crew of the *Clan Matheson*, were put to work as well. The work went no quicker for it, but the reinforcement gave some relief to our almost exhausted men. At ten in the evening we stopped work, having taken in 440 tons of coal, filled the bunkers and replenished the deck stores to some extent. In view of the bad quality of the coal and the great heat our achievement was satisfactory. The defects of the Indian coal were first noticed in coaling, but the main defects were revealed when the coal was used in the furnaces. There was no more steaming without smoke—and a cloud of smoke betrays a ship for miles. Further, our coal consumption was far greater, and the boilers and boiler tubes became so dirty that boiler

cleaning, usually necessary every ten days, was
now needed much more often. At that time we
had often to hear the complaints of the boiler-
room engineer, Marine-Ingenieur Haas.

To discontinue the use of this coal and let the
Pontoporos go was impossible, for nobody could
tell when we should meet another collier. The
Pontoporos was our last reserve and therefore
unconditionally necessary. Our Captain, however, had other plans for her, namely, to appoint
a rendezvous to which the collier should go to
await us. As far as I remember, she was to wait
in the neighbourhood of Simalur Island.

It was first necessary to put an adequate guard
on the *Pontoporos*, for the Greek captain could
not be trusted away without control. The first
officer of the *Markomannia* and Vizesteuermann
d. R. Meyer remained at their posts in the *Pontoporos*, which they had held since the capture of
the ship. Their party was formed of one
Maschinist, as leading artificer, four petty officers,
and nine men. Written instructions were sent
on board with them.

The Greek had been assured that he and his
ship would be set free as soon as the *Markomannia* should be able to take over her full
complement of coal from the *Pontoporos*. In this
case he was to receive an adequate sum of money.

When this had been put in order the *Emden*
left. The *Pontoporos* remained behind, and
vanished on the horizon as we steamed away.

We again made for Preparis North Channel.

At about noon on September 17th the *Emden* reached the point of intersection of the two steamer routes Madras to Rangoon and Calcutta to Singapore, and cruised for some hours there without result. At nightfall we proceeded, passed the straits in the night, and altered course for the Bay of Rangoon, the latter city being the capital of Lower Burma and possessing about 180,000 inhabitants.

Our suspense was great as to whether we should be able to capture any ships at the mouth of this harbour, and therefore from daybreak our glasses were scanning the horizon in all directions. The weather had changed and there were many white squalls which, on the horizon, often looked like smoke clouds, so that we were often disappointed. By midday we were getting impatient.

We first sighted a smoke cloud towards four o'clock, to southwards in the direction of the Molucca Straits.

There was no sense in steaming directly towards the ship, and the order was given to cut off her way to Rangoon. It was not easy for her to escape as we had her constantly in sight.

We came up with her at nightfall, and everything was carried out as usual. Lauterbach, who was tireless as prize officer, and Leutnant z. S. Schmidt boarded the stranger with the necessary party.

We were deceived again. It was a neutral, the

Norwegian ship *Dovre*, 3,000 tons, whose captain greeted our officers warmly in German.

Though meeting with a neutral was annoying, it enabled us to get rid of the English crew of the *Clan Matheson* by passing them over to the Norwegian. He declared himself willing to take them for a payment of 100 Mexican dollars (Mexican money is current in Eastern Asia, etc.).

The transfer of the Englishmen to the Norwegian took place in our cutters, and went smoothly, to our mutual satisfaction. In the meantime Lauterbach conversed with the Norwegian captain, who told him all the news we knew already, and in addition the news that he had been examined last night by the searchlight of a warship, and had met an auxiliary cruiser behind Penang. As he professed to come from Penang he was questioned about this harbour, and told us that the French armoured cruisers *Montcalm* and *Duplex* were at that time stationed there.

This news was of no mean importance to us, as it first gave us the idea of our later proceedings against the harbour of Penang. The Norwegian also explained to Lauterbach that he intended to steam slowly so as not to arrive in Rangoon before dawn, and by this time the *Emden* would be far enough away. The Norwegian took his leave just as it became dark.

When Lauterbach and the prize crew were back in the ship the *Emden* took a westerly course. Lauterbach had brought fresh newspapers with

him with the latest news from the theatres of war.
The news of the greatest interest was of course the
doings of the *Emden* in the Bay of Bengal.   The
English papers did not indeed belie our exploits,
but they attempted to quiet the anxious shipping
and commercial circles with the assurance that the
Emden would very shortly disappear, even if she
had not already been sunk by the allied warships.

This piece of boasting made us laugh.   We were
still undestroyed, in spite of the innumerable
allied warships.

Without meaning to, the various wireless stations
gave us useful news.   The station at Diamond
Point told us that gunfire had been heard at
Akyab.   This place lies on the east coast of Burma,
considerably north of Rangoon.

This kind of news was of great use to us, as it
indicated clearly that warships had been sent to
these districts, which we took care to avoid.

Another intercepted message was pathetically
harmless and came about as follows.   Our friend
Q.M.D. had probably been in communication with
some land station.   Another land station had
intercepted the message and wished to know who
" Q.M.D." might be.   A third station broke in
with the answer : " Q.M.D. is the armoured cruiser
Hampshire " !

We naturally rejoiced at this disclosure, and it
was flattering to us, for the news confirmed our
suspicions that it might be the *Hampshire*.

On September 19th the weather was again so

favourable that the *Markomannia* received the order : " Come alongside for coaling."

The principal reason was that we had stowage room for coal in the *Emden*, and for a warship which may at any minute meet hostile warships it was absolutely necessary to have as much coal on board as possible. We could not know when there would be another opportunity to coal.

Coaling lasted from seven o'clock in the morning till about three in the afternoon, about 310 tons of coal being taken in. We steamed as on September 16th, but this time the *Markomannia* was working her engines and the *Emden* had hers stopped.

In all, we had now 900 tons of coal on board the *Emden*. In spite of the terrible heat the men worked magnificently, but were very worn out and it was necessary that the next night should be one of rest.

As we were not now on any steamer route the night passed without disturbance.

Towards evening we passed through Preparis South Channel, between the Andaman Islands, and full war watches were therefore set.

In the night the *Hampshire's* wireless was so loud that our wireless staff estimated she could not be more than ten sea miles distant.

After midnight we were through the southern straits and altered our course for Madras.

Madras is the capital of the Presidency of Madras, the most important town on the east coast of India, and the third biggest port of India, with

517,335 inhabitants. The town is the seat of the Governor, and lies along the flat beach for about fifteen miles with a breadth of six miles. On the beach in the middle of the town lies the old Fort St. George. The harbour itself is surrounded by a large mole and in the south end of the harbour lie the oil and petroleum tanks of the Burma Oil Company.

The principal object of our visit was to unsettle the Indian inhabitants. In addition we wished to destroy the oil tanks, and if possible the shipping lying in the harbour.

September 20th was a Sunday and after Divine Service the men were allowed to rest all day.

The officers not on duty either sat in the ward-room playing cards or occupied themselves with reading the latest English papers. On the basis of the news in these papers the first officer that afternoon gave a lecture to the petty officers and men about the events of the war.

On September 21st we had a big action-stations practice, supervised by the Captain in person. Owing to lack of opportunity we had not had such a practice for a long time and the day seemed specially favourable for it, especially in view of the raid on Madras next day, where we were liable to meet an enemy warship.

In any case we had to reckon that our fire would be answered by the St. George battery. From our nautical handbooks we found that this battery consisted of 5·9 in. guns. Although they would be of old construction—we assumed this at least, for the fort dated from the 'eighties—5·9 in. shells were not to be under-estimated against our lightly armoured cruiser. Even if they were completely up to date, however, the decision had been made and the plan must, and should, be carried out.

The surprise would indeed be in our favour and we would be able to hinder the English activities with our very powerful searchlights. Also the proverb is not spoken in vain: " Who ventures wins."

CHAPTER VI

IN the annals of the war we find under September 22nd, 1914, the following remarks : " A heroic action was performed on September 22nd, by the German submarine U.9, Kapitänleutnant Otto Weddigen. About twenty sea miles north-west of the Hook of Holland he sank the three English cruisers *Crecy*, *Aboukir* and *Hogue*, and escaped without damage to Wilhelmshaven."

Under the same date we read about the *Emden* : " Later the German light cruiser *Emden* is also noteworthy. From September 10th onwards she made war on British merchant shipping in the Bay of Bengal and caused damage to the English flag to the extent of over 20 million marks."

Then come the names and descriptions of the individual ships. It goes on : " When therefore the *Emden* on September 22nd also set fire by gunfire to the oil tanks of the Burma Oil Company in Madras, and escaped in spite of the fire from the fort, still more anxiety was aroused in England."

The Times says that the courage of the German cruiser deserves recognition, for both officers and men must be aware that sooner or later the cruiser must be caught and shot to pieces. Escape is simply impossible.

The *Daily Chronicle* writes : " The *Emden* has had a momentous cruise. The ship's company have proved their gallantry. We admire the sportsmanship shown in their exploits as much as we heartily wish that the ship may be soon taken."

Thus for the news in the war records. Let us return now to the *Emden* and see what actually happened in the attack on Madras.

I should like to emphasise beforehand that the official news usually sounds far more contemptible than that composed later, with all the éclat possible, by those who were not present at the battle.

September 22nd, 1914, brought us a really beautiful day, such as is only to be experienced in the tropics. We had plenty of work all day. First of all inflammable articles were transferred below the armoured deck. A larger supply of live ammunition was placed ready for the guns.

After lunch an officers' council took place, held by the first officer. It was necessary to go over once more all the points of our duties in the ship, and to give every officer instructions, in case the Captain and first officer should fall in the attack on Madras.

Every possibility must be reckoned with. The men were given an opportunity of bathing in fresh water, and were ordered to put on clean clothes. These measures were purely hygienic, designed to ensure that the men should be clean, so that in case of a wound there should be no complications. This foresight was doubly necessary in the tropics, as in these hot zones the danger of gangrene is far greater than in European or continental climates.

Towards evening the *Markomannia* was detached at an appointed spot. She signalled us : " Wish you the best of success."

And now we were alone once more.

At nightfall our fourth funnel was set. The engines were all clear for full speed, i.e. all boilers had steam up, so that full speed could be used at will.

Towards eight o'clock the Madras light came in sight. We were astounded that this was still burning, proving the unwatchfulness of the English authorities. They cannot have expected, and must have taken it to be impossible, that a fortified harbour should be attacked by " impudent Germans."

Well ! So much the better for us : for surprise was in this case our best ally.

On approaching the town we had another surprise. The harbour lights were all burning, and the whole town was a sea of light.

How different it was in Germany and on German coasts, where at the beginning of war all lights and lighthouses were extinguished, and no coastal town showed a light towards the sea.

Here, however, the opposite was the case.

Towards nine o'clock we came so close that the order to clear ship for action was given. The searchlights, guns, etc., were manned at once. As there was little probability that the torpedo weapons would come into action, I stayed for a time with my friend Levetzow in the after-battery, for I naturally wished to see something of such a splendid undertaking.

My estimate, that no torpedoes would be fired, was fully confirmed.

We rushed towards the harbour at a speed of 17 knots, steering, thanks to their lights, so that at the order " Open fire " the oil tanks and the battery would be in line.

At a quarter-to-ten we were still about 3,000 yards from the land. The *Emden* then turned to port and stopped.

Immediately afterwards followed the orders : " Switch on foremost searchlight. Open fire." A stirring moment !

A few seconds later the first salvo blazed out, and salvo after salvo followed.

The first shots went too far, but the next found their billets and tongues of flame went up from the oil tanks. One shell struck a steamer lying at the mole. Levetzow and I were very anxious about the return fire from the English battery, but to our astonishment not a shot was fired. A few shells fell, however, about 100 yards too far from us, though we could not tell exactly the direction of fire. In my opinion there must have been a gun on the mole, as this was roughly the direction from which the shells came.

This was our baptism of fire. I admit I had imagined something livelier. Our *Emden* was preserved from being hit.

When 125 rounds had been fired the Captain ordered : " Cease fire ! "

The results of this night-shooting were that all the oil tanks had been set alight, a few shells had done some damage in the town, and one ship had been slightly damaged. A few inhabitants were killed unintentionally, as the attack was only directed at essential objects.

It was very lucky for Madras that the wind was westerly so that the flames from the oil tanks stood out seawards. If the opposite had been the case part of the town might easily have been destroyed by the flames.

The moral effect of our enterprise was not at all bad. We learnt later from the papers that a large number of the inhabitants left the town next day by rail. It must have made an incredibly strong impression.

After the cease-fire the searchlights were extinguished, and all electric lights were directed to port. We were thus fully visible as we steamed on a fictitious course northwards. It was particularly necessary to mislead the enemy at this point. If we had at once taken our proper course it is certain that we should shortly have had enemy warships on our tracks.

We steamed northward for a short time, then extinguished all lights and proceeded southwards.

The night passed without the least disturbance. The fire we had kindled burnt, like a great torch, the whole night through on the horizon. Even next morning, at a distance of about sixty sea miles, we could see the huge smoke clouds from the burning oil, a sign that our work was completing itself with certainty.

On September 23rd, in the early morning, we again met the *Markomannia*, whose ship's company were given a short account of our success.

CHAPTER VII

BETWEEN five and six o'clock in the morning we passed the French harbours of Pondicherry and Cuddalore. We had hoped to surprise some ships in the roads, which were quite open, but our hopes were disappointed.

As there was nothing for us in this neighbourhood we sought other fields for our activity. We had, indeed, so thoroughly searched the Bay of Bengal that we could expect nothing more. In many places the anxiety of the English went so far that some harbours completely lost their trade, e.g. Rangoon and the Burmese Peninsula. This was completely blocked for fourteen days, and nothing entered or left.

We shook hands over this news, for where was the English fleet, mistress of the seas? Nowhere was a representative of it to be found.

Our next objective was the island of Ceylon. We intended to steam past it at a suitable distance and board any ships we met.

When we officers were sitting in the wardroom two wishes were freely expressed—that the first ship we met should have the best Cardiff coal on board, and the second the latest newspapers.

The *Emden* was in great need of good coal, for

the stock in the *Markomannia* was diminished, and the use of the pitiable stuff from the *Pontoporos* caused us all some anxiety. Whoever has had to work with such coal will understand that we had no enthusiasm for it. The daily prayer of our suffering engineer, Ellenbroek, was : " May we soon surprise an Admiralty ship with Cardiff coal."

I had a feeling that we should come across such a ship and answered him : " Herr Oberingenieur ! I guarantee that within a few days we shall come upon a Cardiff collier." And so it fell out !

It may sound funny, but it is a rare occurrence that a number of men should have such a feeling and be deceived. My answer proceeded from the fact that there must be many colliers on their way to Singapore and Hong-Kong, as the English warships there had to be provided with good coal. Why should we not have the luck to capture one of them ?

On September 24th we found ourselves on our beat. In the evening very active wireless was heard, but in cipher, so that we could only tell that two warships were communicating with each other not very far from us.

In the hope that ships would be found more plentiful along the coast than at sea, on September 25th we went nearer to Ceylon. At about noon the high mountains of South Ceylon came in sight with their beautiful and varied scenery.

We cruised along the coast at a distance of twenty nautical miles, at a great advantage, as any steamer coming towards us must be seen by us, but we could not be seen from the coast. We were again steaming with good Shantung coal which was very valuable to us owing to the small amount of smoke produced.

We drew nearer to the steamship route Colombo-Penang-Singapore, the most important in the whole of the Indian Ocean, linking England with her East Asiatic possessions.

Soon after lunch we sighted a smoke cloud right ahead. Without increasing speed we approached the ship slowly but surely.

On nearing her we found that she was flying the English commercial ensign, whereupon we hoisted our own.

I would gladly have seen the long faces of the Englishmen. The *Emden* went quite close to her, and then ordered her to stop. Lauterbach and Leutnant z. S. Schmidt went on board with the prize crew, carried on as usual and announced as follows : " English ship *King Lud*, 3,650 tons, without cargo, from Suez to Calcutta." (79° 46' E., 5° 47' N.)

As the ship was to be sunk at once the torpedo officer and the blasting party went on board the prize.

What we took from the *King Lud* was the splendid supply of stores, and especially meal and potatoes, which were of great value to us.

In order that the proper branch should carry out the work, the steward and his men also went on board the *King Lud*.

In an hour we had everything transferred and the English ship's company were sent to the *Markomannia*, who in the meantime had received her military commando under Kapitänleutnant Klöpper.

Towards four o'clock in the afternoon the *King Lud* was so disabled that she could be left to the mercy of the waters. Her last voyage into the deep could be watched as the *Emden* proceeded on her way.

Our orders were that we were to pass Colombo in darkness, as Colombo was one of the largest transit harbours in the East.

Towards eight in the evening we were about thirty miles south of Colombo. The English here apparently did not wish to repeat the mistake of Madras. Searchlights were continually playing over the horizon, and it was to be assumed with certainty that there would be ships patrolling outside the harbour.

An hour later we sighted a ship to port, steaming with all lights burning.

The *Emden* made towards her, and the *Marko-mannia* kept to her previous course. On nearer approach we made out a large tank ship, which, like all her kind, had a funny appearance, carrying her funnel right aft.

Overtaking her from the stern we hailed her

with the megaphone, and asked for her nationality. The answer came : " Norwegian steamship
Oceanis."

As we had no wish to be recognised the *Emden*
hastened to answer : " Proceed, good voyage ! "
and we steamed back at full speed behind the
Markomannia.

Our next objective was a small island west of
Colombo with a lighthouse serving as a guiding
light for that port, on the steamship route from
Colombo to Minicoy. Every ship coming from
the west and entering Colombo passes Minicoy.

Towards ten o'clock the lights of a ship were
sighted on the starboard bow. One got the
impression that she had come straight out of the
harbour of Colombo. She was shown up well
by the searchlights.

We proceeded quietly along our previous course,
as we were bound to meet the ship at a safe distance from the harbour. An hour later it was
possible to hail her (79° 21′ E., 7° 10′ W.).
Lauterbach and I were sent over with the prize
crew. When we came on board we acquainted
ourselves at once with her name, cargo and
destination. She was the 3,500 ton English ship
Tymeric, with 4,000 tons of sugar *en route* for
England—a fine cargo to sweeten the sea water !

First this ship had to follow the *Emden*, so that
the sinking should not take place within a certain
distance of the gates of Colombo. As usual, it
was intended to give the crew an opportunity to

9

pack up their personal belongings. This could not, however, be carried out.

When Lauterbach told the captain his fate and ordered him to follow the *Emden*, both the captain and the chief engineer refused.

What now? Naturally, Lauterbach reported these events to the Captain of the *Emden*.

Hardly had this happened when an unusual scene was enacted on the *Tymeric*. The captain, in a rage at having run into our hands right outside Colombo, and in sight of the searchlights of that harbour, began to curse the Germans with the words: " Damned Germans ! "

There was no more palaver! With such a fellow the short way was the only way, and Lauterbach accordingly signalled to report these insults and ask for permission to sink the ship at once.

This permission was at once granted, and in addition men were sent over from the *Emden* to reinforce the prize crew in the *Tymeric*. The captain and his chief engineer were brought over to the *Emden*. On account of the sudden alteration in the conditions it was not possible to allow the *Tymeric's* men any time to pack their things. The English crew were quickly transferred to the *Markomannia*.

I was present when the captain expressed a wish to pack up his belongings. There was very little time, and he could only pack his mess jacket and a few underclothes, for which he had specially asked. On the one hand he deserved this treatment for his cursing, but at the same time I was sorry for him, knowing that all his personal things must be a prey to the waves. In this case a strict example had to be made, especially as, after capture, the captain and his ship were under German martial law. His anger at being attacked so close to the port of Colombo I could understand, and especially his anger at the naval staff in Colombo who, as the irate captain explained, had guaranteed with all certainty that the coast was clear. He had his countrymen to thank for this erroneous advice. We were not answerable for it.

The English crew naturally had a grievance against their captain, whose fault it was that they lost their possessions. Their oaths to make him suffer for it at the first opportunity were understandable and pleasant hearing.

The Englishmen were scarcely on board the *Markomannia* when everything was clear for sinking the *Tymeric*. First, however, the abundance of fresh provisions discovered were transferred to the boats and a rapid but effective search was made for newspapers of recent date. This day's newspapers were specially interesting for us on account of the news of the *Emden*.

While Lauterbach and I were carrying out our duties with the prize crew in the *Tymeric*, the *Emden* had sighted another ship. It could, however, be assumed that this was the Dutch mail steamer *Konigin Emma*, who had announced her arrival in Colombo by wireless for about this time. The *Emden*, therefore, let her go unchallenged.

As already stated the captain and the engineer had been taken from the *Tymeric* to the *Emden* under restraint, and a place was prepared for them on the middle deck. Later they were given lodging in the Minenhellegat (space where the mine gear was prepared). A guard was placed over them, carrying side-arms.

After the *Konigin Emma* had passed the *Tymeric* in the distance, Levetzow reported that everything was clear for sinking in the latter.

I returned to the *Emden* with the prize crew, and after a successful explosion, Levetzow and his party did so as well. We did not wait for the *Tymeric* to sink, but proceeded at once on the previous course.

Although it was past midnight our officers at once rushed for the newspapers. They contained plenty of news of the war at home—very garbled reports. We were most interested in the reports of our doings in Madras, for we were now learning for the first time how the enemy regarded our activities.

The papers were principally occupied with the damage done, for which the figure of 20 million gold marks was given, a fairly large sum for the destruction of the tanks and the burnt oil. Later reports stated that the inhabitants in large numbers were leaving for the interior, many of them travelling on the roofs of the railway carriages.

We could only wish that the feeling of insecurity and the mood of unrest might spread to the interior of India. The papers freely blamed the inactivity of the Allied warships, and expressed the opinion that with such a number of cruisers they should have been able to dispose of the *Emden*.

For the *Emden* herself, and for Kapitän von Müller, there was nothing but praise. The papers talked enthusiastically of " fair play," and said that the Captain of the *Emden* must be a real sportsman—great praise from English mouths, for in England sport is of national interest.

There were a large number of articles about the *Emden*, all with more or less the same opinions. One paper was particularly witty. It had among the advertisements one of a common soap, with the legend : " The soap is so good that even the *Emden* took it from the *Indus*, and used it." Certainly an unusual advertisement, but I am firmly convinced that among the English it would be fully appreciated.

We were still searching the papers, and the clock showed the first hour after midnight, when suddenly there was a night alarm.

A new victim was in sight, and a proof that we were on the right route. Lauterbach and Leutnant z. S. Zimmermann were sent over with the prize crew. The order was given that our officers were to take command of the new prize at once, and were to follow the *Emden*.

We were naturally very curious to learn the nationality of the ship that had fallen into our hands. She was the 4,437 ton English steamship *Gryfevale*, from Aden to Colombo, without cargo.

Our Captain at once came to the decision to use this ship as a dump.

When all was clear, the previous course for Minicoy was resumed.

On September 26th, at dawn, the look out sighted a Dutchman passing at a great distance, which was very agreeable for us, as we did not wish to be recognised in this neighbourhood. As the Dutchman was equipped with wireless it would have been easy for her by broadcasting the news of our whereabouts to put enemy cruisers on our tracks in a short time. Towards noon the smoke cloud caused by the Dutchman vanished on the horizon. Probably we had not been recognised.

Soon afterwards we intercepted a wireless call from an English ship asking the Dutchman if he had seen anything of the *Emden*. The Dutchman's answer, which we intercepted at the same time, set our minds at rest. It ran: " For reasons of neutrality, answer refused." It is still not clear to me whether the Dutchman recognised us. In any case he conducted himself correctly as a neutral.

Intercepted wireless messages announced a Danish motor-ship *Fionia*, which towards evening

steamed past us clearly lighted as befits a large
passenger-steamer. We did not trouble her in
any way. Lauterbach and the captain of the
Gryfevale were of the opinion that the Dane was a
British India liner. However that might be our
Captain had no desire to chase an unknown and
very fast ship, which in addition was going to
Colombo.

Early on September 27th, about three o'clock,
a ship was again sighted coming towards us,
which seemed from her lights to be a merchant
vessel. On nearer approach the look out suddenly
announced that behind the lighted ship was
another steaming without lights. " Clear ship for
Action " was at once ordered, and we sheered off
to port. We had no desire to fall into any such
trap. Thank heaven ! The supposed mysterious
darkened ship was a dark smoke cloud which the
stranger had thrown out, probably while cleaning
fires and stoking up again. This solution was
welcome and assured us that we were not running
into an enemy warship. It gave us freedom of
action with regard to the new arrival, which was
halted as usual.

Levetzow and Gyssling went on board with the
prize crew and announced : " English steamship
Buresk, 4,350 tons, cargo 6,600 tons first-class
Cardiff coal, chartered by the English Admiralty,
from England to Hong-Kong."

This announcement caused great joy in the
Emden. Here we had the long-desired good coal,

and better we could not wish for. Most pleased of all was our suffering engineer, who almost fell on my neck since it was I who had prophesied this prize. This collier, priceless to us, was captured 76° 41′ E., 7° 24′ N.

We were now provided with coal for a long time ahead. As the *Markomannia* must soon be completely empty, it was decided to appoint the *Buresk* a follower, and what was still more in our favour was that the *Buresk* could steam at least ten knots. I learnt later that this ship did on occasion achieve twelve knots, but I cannot confirm this with certainty.

Since August 6th the gallant *Markomannia* had faithfully accompanied us, and had done us good service in many ways. When we knew that the *Buresk* had 1,600 tons more coal than the *Markomannia* had on leaving Tsingtau, our hopes of being able to rely on her for some time were considerably increased, provided that no misfortune overtook the *Emden*. It was intended, as far as possible, to exhaust the coal in the *Markomannia* and then abandon her.

To carry out our plans for the future the *Buresk* had to be properly manned. Kapitänleutnant Klöpper was given command of this ship, with Leutnants z. S. Schmidt and Gyssling as watch-officers. Torpedomaschinist Wittkopf, whom we had taken over from the *Kormoran* in Tsingtau to make up our war complement, was chief engineer. Two maschinistenmaaten, two seamen, and three stokers were also sent over. The Arab crew of the *Buresk* was retained, which was useful to us for two reasons : first, because we did not need to send over too many of our own people, and secondly because it was desirable to have a thoroughly trained crew for our new companion.

All the English crews, who had hitherto been accommodated in the *Markomannia*, were transferred to the *Gryfevale*, our dump. The Englishmen from the *Buresk* were to have been transferred to the dump, but a request came from the captain and chief engineer for permission to accompany the *Emden* in the *Buresk*.

Our Captain had nothing against it, but, as often happens, one request was followed by others. Of the *Buresk's* people the second engineer, an English steward, and the Norwegian ship's cook made the same request through their captain.

What has been said to A must also be said to B, and in this case this could be done without anxiety. These people could not be at all dangerous, and in addition they were watched by our own people among the crew of the *Buresk*. We did not quite understand this request, for these men would now remain strictly prisoners of war. I would prefer freedom. An old sea dog, however, cannot so easily separate himself from the floating home that was once his own, and a certain feeling of home and of dependence on the ship would drive him to such a request.

With Levetzow's return we proceeded on our way. The order of steaming was again the famous echelon, with the *Buresk* to port, to starboard the *Gryfevale*, and behind her the *Markomannia*.

September 27th was a beautiful day, whose clear weather and mirror-like sea made our cruise particularly pleasant. In the morning, as almost invariably happened on Sunday, Divine Service was held, and a short description of Divine Service on board is here introduced.

As there is no parson on light cruisers, Divine Service is held by the senior Protestant naval officer present, who in this case was the Captain. After Divisions, church was piped by the boots-mannmaate (boatswain's mate), i.e. the necessary signals were given with the boatswain's pipe, and the Protestant part of the ship's company who were not at the time on duty assembled on the middle deck, aft. The band played a hymn, and then followed readings from the Bible with explanations, the Lord's Prayer, and in conclusion another hymn. For the Catholics, God's service was held at the same time in the forecastle. It was held by the senior Catholic officer, and in our case this was the adjutant, Leutnant z. S. von Guerard, who, however, was usually on duty in the wireless room, so that as a general substitute I had to hold the service. The Epistle and Gospel were read, followed by meditation and prayers.

As far as was possible the whole was given a ceremonial character, though the ceremony was not elaborate, as there was little room on board, and there was not much time for preparations. We had to be content. Of good-will there was plenty, and thus it was possible in such devotions to give the men spiritual edification. Our Captain placed great importance on Sunday Divine Service, as it gave the Lord's Day a different character from weekdays. Strenuous work could naturally not always be avoided, and we were at war, which remains war and cannot be treated as peace.

After Divine Service the men were allowed to go off duty as far as possible, but this could not always be accomplished. Only too often a ship would interfere, needing for prize, search, blasting, and sinking parties a large number of men. I think, however, that to the majority of our men a prize was quite as agreeable as freedom.

September 27th, a Sunday, had begun well and looked like going on well—a day of rest in beautiful weather, when a signal came from Lauterbach in the *Gryfevale* : " The captured ships' companies are making trouble through drunkenness. Some fighting. Have put a number of men in irons. Urgently request reinforcement."

Now where was our Sunday's rest ?

Lauterbach's humanity, which had induced him to allow some Englishmen to take drinks with them from their ships—whisky was naturally the favourite—was well rewarded.

Lauterbach was ordered to confiscate the liquor at once. I think there was not much left. The

Emden then went quite near to the *Gryfevale* so as to be able to speak directly with Lauterbach by megaphone.

The excitement in the *Gryfevale* soon subsided. The captains apologised to Lauterbach for their men and there the matter ended. The *Gryfevale* took up her previous place and we hoped to get a little of our Sunday's rest after all.

We had just sat down to our luxurious midday meal, of which the menu read : " Soup, corned beef with rice, stewed fruit," when some disturbance became noticeable, owing to the increased speed of the ship. The *Emden* was steaming at full speed and that was sufficient alarm for us. The soup was left standing and we all ran to the bridge or the quarterdeck to see what was happening this time.

The usual smoke cloud was seen and soon a steam-ship with one funnel appeared on the horizon.

In the *Emden* the prize crew and search party were piped away, and the duty cutter's crew, that of the port cutter. Oberleutnant z. S. Geerdes, and Leutnant z. S. Schall, were appointed to deal with the new-comer.

When we were near enough the stranger was ordered to stop and the prize crew sent across.

It was the 3,500 ton English steamship *Ribera*, in ballast (75° 26′ E., 7° 30′ N.). The only thing useful to the *Emden* was the

The buckled Deck and Funnel of the "Emden"

plentiful provisions, and a very complete signal book. Part of the provisions the *Emden* took, and the rest, with the English ship's company, was transferred to the *Gryfevale*.

This time Kapitänleutnant Gaede was to employ his guns once more, and with a few well-placed shells the *Ribera* was dispatched to the " eternal hunting grounds."

This time everything went smoothly, and the ship sunk very quickly.

Now as to the signal book. Our latest victim, on her last voyage in the Indian Ocean, had met with an English troop transport, which was on its way to Aden. This consisted of sixty-seven to seventy ships, protected by the English battle-ship *Swiftsure*, of the Indian station, and the Russian armoured cruiser *Askold*. The *Ribera* had exchanged signals with both these ships.

After the sinking of the *Ribera* our course was set again for Minicoy.

We hoped, indeed, to surprise a few ships on the way, but had a feeling that it was time to vanish, as it was very necessary for us to coal again.

At nightfall : " Steamship in sight on the starboard bow," was again reported.

The *Emden* allowed the new victim to approach quietly, and Levetzow and Fikentscher, with their party, and Marine-Ingenieur Haas with the blasting party were sent over. Levetzow sig-nalled at once : " English steamship *Foyle*, 4,147 tons, without cargo from Aden to Colombo." (47° 5′ E., 7° 56′ N.).

This ship was to be made clear for sinking straight away when a brightly lighted ship was sighted, and Levetzow was ordered to follow with the *Foyle*. The *Emden* with her conspicuous train, consisting of *Markomannia, Buresk, Gryfevale*, and *Foyle*, approached the new victim.

The many lights raised joyful hopes of a rich mail packet, possibly carrying money, and therefore Zahlmeister-applikant (accountant officer) Bordeaux was added to the prize crew under command of Geerdes and Schall, as teller, if a large sum should be captured.

The report from the ship we had stopped was a severe disappointment. A mail packet, but a Dutchman, and therefore to be released at once as a neutral. The ship was the *Djocja*, and belonged to the Batavia line. Geerdes and Schall were able to buy from her some good cigarettes, which were all exhausted in the *Emden*. These were naturally much envied by the rest, as the supply was so small that it was only enough for the two officers mentioned.

Meantime Levetzow had made the *Foyle* clear for sinking. The crew had packed up their personal belongings and were transferred to the *Gryfevale*.

When the blasting cartridges had been fired, Levetzow and his party returned to the *Emden*, and the *Foyle* was left to her fate.

The two prisoners from the *Tymeric* were transferred to the *Gryfevale* this Sunday, and Lauterbach and his party returned to the *Emden*.

The *Gryfevale* herself was abandoned about noon, after the Englishmen, to our great surprise, had given three cheers each for our Captain, the officers, and the *Emden*. She made for Colombo, while we went south towards the Maldives.

CHAPTER VIII

THE 28th September found us on a southerly course, as it was necessary to get as far as possible from the scene of our latest activities. There could be no doubt that the non-arrival at Colombo of the ships we had sunk would awaken suspicion and if the English should learn where we had last been busy they would certainly send after us a number of warships. Disappearance and secrecy were therefore urgent necessities for us.

The need for coaling also forced the *Emden* to seek some unfrequented neighbourhood.

In the afternoon the *Emden* was cleared for coaling, and the day passed in complete peace. This was welcomed by the ship's company, especially as the destruction of the second set of ships had meant working day and night.

On September 29th it was our intention to take in coal under the protection of the Maldive Islands. In the early morning a party was sent over to the *Markomannia* to clear her for coaling. The advantage of this preparation lay in the fact that the *Emden* had only to go alongside and coaling could begin.

At eight in the morning the islands came in

sight, and towards eleven the *Emden* and her
train were navigating the various straits which
separate the Maldive Islands. We then went
alongside the *Markomannia* and made fast, and
the coaling itself began about noon. The *Emden's*
engines were stopped, and the *Markomannia's*
were moving sufficiently to give us steerage way.

Coaling continued till eleven in the evening.
Five hundred and seventy tons were taken in by
the *Emden*, which is certainly not much, but the
heat made it impossible to do more. The *Emden*
then cast off and cruised in the neighbourhood,
as the next day was also to be used for coaling.
The night passed without disturbance.

September 30th was a day of parting, as the
Markomannia was to be abandoned. In the
early morning our new companion, the *Buresk*,
made fast alongside the *Markomannia* and took
over the stores of oil and fresh water. The men
were given the opportunity to send letters home
as the *Markomannia* was to make for a port in
the Dutch Indies and would be able to deliver
the mail. Naturally the men were strictly forbidden to write about the doings of the *Emden*.
Secrecy was so important that some control had
to be exercised, and the officers, therefore, had
the " pleasure " of reading the letters of the
Emden's men in the capacity of censors.

The officers themselves had barely written
their letters when the letters of the men began
to pour in. Many howlers came to light which

were very laughable. It was pleasant and refreshing to see in all the letters the enthusiasm of the men for their duties, and how proud they were of belonging to the *Emden*. There were no complaints of hard work or bad food. Almost every letter contained the wish for further successes against the enemies of the Fatherland. In view of the enthusiasm in the men's letters the irritation at having to act as censors was turning to pleasure. Our labour was its own refreshment. It was a pleasure to work with such a ship's company and the results of the censorship was a renewed and enthusiastic confidence in the trustworthiness and capability of our men.

Everyone naturally wrote in the hope that the letter would reach home, but this hope was not very secure for the *Markomannia* might easily be attacked by enemy ships, and it was, further, uncertain whether these letters would be allowed to go through.

I learnt later that only a few of these letters reached their destinations.

At about two o'clock the *Emden* went alongside the *Markomannia*. The work of coaling was begun again, and lasted till about half-past seven in the evening. By this time we had again a thousand tons on board.

Zahlmeisterapplikant Bordeaux went over to the *Markomannia* with the *Emden's* mail and £50 in English money. His errand was to buy the things needed for the *Emden* in some neutral port.

The *Markomannia* was first to meet the *Pontoporos*, fill up with coal from her, and run for some port in the Dutch Indies where she was to take in as many provisions as possible, leave secretly and steam to an appointed rendezvous to wait for the *Emden*. We reckoned on meeting her again at the beginning of November, and she therefore had four weeks to spare.

It was hard to part from our faithful companion under the tried command of Kapitän Faass, for the *Markomannia* had shared the *Emden's* joy and sorrow for over two months, had remained faithful, and had helped us as much as possible.

The question naturally arose as to whether we should meet again. How easy it would be for some harm to come either to the *Emden* or the *Markomannia*.

Such doleful thoughts, however, did not depress us for long. Our powers are increased if we face the future cheerfully.

The parting from the *Markomannia* took place towards half-past eight in the evening. Her ship's company gave three cheers for the *Emden*.

We never saw her again. She rests at the bottom of the sea.

As long as the *Markomannia* was still in sight we cruised up and down, and only afterwards altered course for our new objective, the Chagos Archipelago.

This destination was decided on for two reasons.

First it was important, and indeed necessary, to vanish for a time from the scene of our former activities, not only on account of the enemy, but because our ship needed overhauling. It was, of course, not possible to dock her, but by canting some of the encrustments, composed of small mussels attached to the ship's bottom, could be cleared off. They encourage rust and detract from the ship's speed.

Part of the ship was also to be repainted. The gallant *Emden* had at this time a savage aspect, on account of the length of service at sea and the frequent coaling. Of the paint, once so perfect, nothing was to be seen. The life-rails were in most places bent by the weight of the deck stores of coal. On the quarterdeck there was practically no linoleum left. There could be no question of replacement, for the necessary reserves had been put ashore at Tsingtau. We comforted ourselves with the thought that the beauty of the ship did not matter in war time so much as the fitness of the ship's company and the constant readiness of all guns and torpedo tubes.

The engines, also, however, needed overhauling. As far as possible Oberingenieur Ellenbroek, Ingenieur Haas, and Ingenieur Andresen for the electrical machines, had already seen to this. Ingenieur Stoffers was still ill, and therefore, to his great regret could take no part. He was the one case which gave our two doctors, Stabsarzt Dr. Luther and Assistenarzt Dr. Schwabe, any trouble. Otherwise the health on board was more than satisfactory.

The second part of the plan for our cruise to the Chagos Archipelago was concerned with the war on merchant shipping.

The steamship routes from Australia to Suez and from Mauritius to Calcutta pass this archipelago to the southward. According to the declaration of the captain of the *Ribera* the troops in transport from Australia to Europe must pass this way. To surprise such a transport by night would be good sport for us. In addition this was also the route followed by the meat ships from Australia to England. We had been in need of fresh meat for some time. A capture would have been of great benefit to us, and at the same time have reduced the supply for England.

We cruised slowly towards the two steamship routes—slowly because the *Emden* had only four boilers in action, the others being in the process of being refitted. The weak point, the tubes, were changed as far as possible. A thorough overhaul of the auxiliary machinery was also going on and the engines were therefore stopped alternately. A very important part of the ship, the condensers, were thoroughly cleaned. These are the machines that remove the salt from the feed-water. If salt settled on the tubes of this machine it had to be scraped off from time to time, and if this was not done regularly the feed-

water would not be freed from salt. In the
engines themselves the washers were examined,
and when worn were replaced by new ones. The
engineering staff had work enough.

The sailors had to begin to refit the body of the
ship. For example, new lines had to be fitted to
the life-boats for hoisting and lowering them.

On the whole, however, the ship's company
were given as much free time as possible. The
men had time to repair their clothes and belongings. New clothes and underclothes were also
issued from the store to some extent.

Our military duties, however, were also not
forgotten. The hand arms, usually carefully
stowed away, were taken out and cleaned, and the
machine guns, usually kept under the armoured
deck, were set in order and their crews were given
an opportunity to make themselves familiar with
their weapons. Infantry exercises, at all events
as far as the size of the ship permitted, were carried out frequently and included wheeling and
general evolutions.

Finally there was gunnery practice. The
Buresk towed a target at which shortened ammunition was fired. There were also action evolutions supervised by the Captain. The enemy
was naturally represented by the *Buresk*.

In these evolutions the reserves were also given
training ; thus, the stokers were given practice
on the guns. For emergencies this was of the
greatest importance, for our principal weapon,

the guns, had to be in as good practice as possible, so that as each man fell out the firing could be continued. Next to these men in importance came the magazine's crews, and this was perhaps our weakest point, for the ammunition could not be brought to the guns under cover and so in a fight heavy losses were to be reckoned on at this point. The greatest number of reserves had to be trained for this duty. In our last fight, on November 9th, 1914, our experiences in this matter were bitter, for it was owing to the ammunition not being got to the guns in sufficient quantities, that we were so easily and quickly dealt with. Our light cruisers, with the exception of the newest, were not built for cruiser warfare, but for foreign cruising, and that not in tropical climates. Later, in captivity, Kapitän von Müller and we worked out together a new type of cruiser for foreign stations. The basic condition of this new type was stronger guns. We had only 4·1 in. quick-firers, whereas 5·9 in. guns were necessary on all counts. Another point of importance was better armour on the sides. The cruiser was also to have favourably placed and well protected ammunition approaches, as well as more powerful engines and boilers to take both coal and oil fuel. Our position in the *Emden* was that we were inferior to almost every enemy cruiser, both in armament and speed. However much we would have liked to have joined in battle it had to be avoided on these grounds. It was to be expected with 99 per cent. of certainty that in the event of a meeting with an enemy cruiser we would be, if not completely finished, made incapable of further action during the war.

The success of the *Emden* was due to the outstanding qualities of her leader and Captain, but it must be mentioned in the same breath that the splendid spirit and readiness for sacrifice of the *Emden's* men were of inestimable value to her Captain.

A week was usefully employed in the manner above described.

At about seven in the morning of October 9th we ran into the harbour of Diego Garcia, the southernmost island of the Chagos Archipelago.

This miniature fairyland consists of coral banks, covered in high palms, and the value of the islands lies in cocoanut oil and copra. The sheltered bay cannot be seen from the sea and was therefore particularly suitable for our ends.

The *Emden* passed carefully through the narrow entrance into the harbour, and the *Buresk* followed and anchored in our immediate vicinity.

The anchor had scarcely touched ground when a party was sent over from the *Emden* to the *Buresk* to prepare for coaling. At the same time some compartments were filled, i.e. water was allowed to run into them so that the *Emden* was given a cant and hove her stern a little out of the water. The scraping of the ship's bottom could thus begin at once. There was an incredible

number of mussels on the bottom and sides of the
ship, and their removal was urgently necessary.
Afterwards the sides had to be scrubbed and
painted with oil paint. Our first officer had
charge of these operations, well seconded by
Bootsmann (boatswain) Müller.

The appearance of two ships in the quiet
harbour was naturally something of an event for
the natives. We might have been lying there
half an hour when a boat rowed by natives approached the *Emden*. It brought on board the
subordinate manager of the Oil Company ex-
ploiting Diego Garcia, who was born in Mada-
gascar and was only master of the French tongue.
The Captain first spoke with this man, who afterwards came into the wardroom and made very
good practice with the iced whisky and soda.
For us the conversation became interesting from
the moment that we recognised that this manager
and the inhabitants had no idea that there was
a war on in the world.

This surprising condition of ignorance was
easily explained. Only once in three months
did a sailing-ship ply between Diego Garcia and
Mauritius. The sailing-ship had not appeared
for a quarter but was expected during the next
few days, and it was therefore clear that the inhabitants could have no idea of the important
events that had been going on in the world.
Since the beginning of July they had had no news
of any kind from the outside world.

This ignorance was welcome to us, for it gave us an opportunity to replenish our stores.

The disadvantage of ignorance, an insatiable hunger for news from the world, was brought thoroughly home to us in the wardroom, for the man questioned the souls out of our bodies. Willingly or not we had to become tellers of fairy tales. We made up a beautiful series of incidents for him.

The oil company manager could not be blamed for wishing to know the reason of our stop at Diego Garcia, in the far South. The excuse made was that urgent repairs forced us to put in to this harbour but they would be completed in two days.

Then the man wanted to know where we were going and what a German ship was doing in the neighbourhood, and we had to find the right answer for this somewhat awkward question. A proper seaman is never at a loss for an answer. Resourcefulness is a rule of life at sea, and the inquisitive oil manager was told that we were taking part in " world manœuvres " in which the united fleets of Germany, England and France had their principal base of operations in the Indian ocean.

We were pleased that the man at once firmly believed us. Then, however, he wanted further news of the world. We answered him evasively that we had been so long at sea that we could hardly remember what was new or old. Perhaps, however, the Herr Unterdirektor did not yet know that Pope Pius X was dead. No, he did not know it, and was not a little delighted with this piece of news.

This pleasant conversation was in full swing when the first manager and chief of the oil company appeared on board, and was invited by the captain to go to the cabin. Here this gentleman also inquired for news, and of course the same dish was served out to him as to his subordinate. There were delicate moments, however, for the first manager, an Englishman, was more inquisitive and less retiring than his subordinate, and he asked the captain why our ship presented such a wild appearance.

Our captain, with an answer always ready, told him a story of a frightful storm from which the ship had only with the greatest difficulty escaped. The credulous first manager said that he had thought so from the appearance of the cruiser.

At the conclusion of this entertainment the manager brought forward a request. With the permission of the Captain the mechanics were to repair his motor-boat for him—a good boat, but rendered useless by the ignorance of the islanders. Could the captain send a few men from the engine-room staff ashore, etc. ?

Kapitän von Müller assented and at once sent Maschinistmaat Kluge, who ran our own motor-boat in time of peace, with some of his men, who in a short time had the manager's boat working again.

The manager was so delighted that he sent a letter inviting Kapitän v. Müller to breakfast on shore. Our captain, however, politely and gratefully declined on account of the exigencies of the service.

It must be admitted that the manager was grateful. He sent a large live pig on board for the wardroom, and for the men an enormous heap of fish, and a whole boatload of fruit.

There was nothing else for it but to accept the gifts. As we did not wish, however, to be under an obligation to our enemies, we sent Spender back a few bottles of wine and whisky and some cigars as an exchange. I think the Diego Garcia people never had such noble givers as guests. As thanks for all this they wished next day to catch lobsters for us. As our time was short we could not wait, a fact which we all rather regretted as we would gladly have seen such a delicacy on our modest table again.

At about two in the afternoon we weighed anchor and made fast alongside the *Buresk* for coaling. Coaling lasted till twelve midnight. As, however, owing to the tropical heat, only 400 tons were taken in by the *Emden*, the next day also was to be employed in coaling. The *Emden* therefore remained alongside and the night passed without disturbance.

On October 10th, at six in the morning, coaling

was continued. At about ten o'clock the thousand tons was complete and the strenuous work ended.

Towards eleven we left the hospitable island, steering a fictitious course to the north-west. Later we altered course to north-east, and cruised for a time along the steamship route Australia to Aden, in the hope of surprising a ship there.

We had no luck, and went west of the Maldives with the intention of proceeding northwards.

Our real plans were to go direct from Diego Garcia to Penang and surprise and destroy by means of torpedoes the warships lying there.

Meantime we succeeded in intercepting a wireless message from an English ship, inquiring about the security of the Colombo to Aden line. The answer, probably from Colombo, said that there was no danger and that the route was again safe for shipping. This brilliantly favourable announcement decided Kapitän von Müller to change his plan and take to this "hunting ground" north of the Maldives. For greater security, however, the *Emden* was to take in as much coal as possible beforehand.

As this was the time of the North-East monsoons (October to March, N.E. ; April to September, S.W.), the *Emden* looked for a quiet place west of the Maldives, but the swell there was so strong that there was no possibility of making fast to the *Buresk*, nor even in the straits between the islands. The east side near to the islands offered enough shelter, but we were not to coal until we reached the end of the Maldive Islands.

The time was again occupied in action evolutions, wheeling, and infantry exercises. Otherwise, however, the men were given as much time as possible in which to get ready for the approaching strenuous work in the new hunting ground.

On October 15th we had reached the Miladu-Madu atoll, almost the most northerly of the Maldives. *Buresk* made fast alongside the *Emden*, with our engines turning over very slowly. Coaling began, in fine weather, at eleven in the forenoon, and 280 tons were taken in. The men worked marvellously, and we made a record for our war cruise, taking in 90 tons in an hour.

When it is remembered how hot it is so close to the Equator, and what difficulties there are in coaling at sea, only the greatest admiration can be expressed for the *Emden's* ship's company. The Captain gave special recognition and thanks to this brilliant effort of the ship's company.

CHAPTER IX

TOWARDS three o'clock the work was finished, and we proceeded in the direction of the island of Minicoy and the shipping routes passing near it.

At half-past ten in the evening the Minicoy light came in sight and it behoved us to be careful, for this light was the principal guiding light for ships approaching Colombo from the west.

The neighbourhood was well known to us as we had rendered it unsafe barely two weeks before. Towards midnight the lights of a steamship came in sight, *en route* probably from Aden to Colombo. The *Emden* went towards her at full speed, intending to approach in the way familiar to the reader, when suddenly dark shapes appeared behind her.

We in the *Emden* believed that the shadow was a warship steaming without lights in order to entrap the enemy, and wheeled about at once. We had experienced something of the same sort shortly before the capture of the *Buresk*, and had therefore become careful. In the *Emden* everything was already clear for action, and the first torpedo officer wished to clear away another torpedo tube, when we discovered the fact that it was a thick smoke cloud. On a dark night it is possible to be deceived, and the greatest care is necessary.

We turned again towards the ship and ordered her to stop (73° 11′ E.; 8° 10′ N.). Lauterbach and Fikentscher were sent over with their party, and the report soon followed : " English ship *Clan Grant*, 3,948 tons, piece goods, from England to Colombo and other Indian ports."

Further reports stated that the valuable cargo consisted of live cattle, flour, cakes, a good quantity of other provisions and quantities of beer and cigarettes.

We were not a little delighted. We could do with such a plentiful addition to our housekeeping supplies, for we had on board only the absolute necessaries. The greatest joy, however, was expressed by our cigarette smokers. The stock of cigarettes, as far as the wardroom was concerned, was my special concern, but for some time our supply had been exhausted, although we had brought a large stock with us and had augmented it later from the *Princess Alice*.

The positively luxurious supplies of provisions of all kinds decided our Captain to give the order for the ship to follow us. In the next few days the *Clan Grant* was to be emptied as much to our advantage as was possible.

We proceeded slowly along a course for Colombo. On October 16th we stopped at seven in the morning, the steam pinnace and some of the boats were at once lowered, and the steward, Färber, with seventeen men, went on board the *Clan Grant*, which was now accordingly emptied. Discovery after discovery—crockery, which we could very well use, table linen, typewriters in positively fantastic numbers, case after case of cigarettes, tools of all sorts, fire-bricks which were urgently necessary for our boilers, oil, live cattle, etc. A big warehouse could not have had a more varied stock than this ship. As there were not only provisions but a large amount of material useful for the ship herself, several other officers were sent on board to represent their own branches.

While we were still hard at work the look-out in the *Emden* reported a smoke cloud in the west. Lauterbach, the very model of a prize officer, was hurriedly recalled from the *Clan Grant*. The *Emden* left her convoy and her boats and steamed towards the smoke cloud.

On nearer approach the matter seemed a little peculiar, and possibly dangerous, for a mast rose above the horizon such as would only be borne by a torpedo-boat or monitor. Also the stern of the ship, which soon came in sight, looked very like the types mentioned. Otherwise the hull was rolling in the swell quite harmlessly, and "Clear ship for Action" had almost been ordered when our mistake was discovered.

Laughter broke over the *Emden* at the discovery, for the stranger which had presented such a martial aspect was now recognised for what it was—a deep-sea dredger! (72° 24′ E., 8° 21′ N.) There was nothing to demand Lauterbach's skill! The order to follow was enough.

With her new victim the *Emden* returned to her convoy.

I would have liked to have seen the faces of those who had stayed behind, when we returned with a dredger captured on the high seas. There was more amusement when Lauterbach and Schall, without the prize crew, went on board the captive. She was the deep-sea dredger *Ponrabbel*, on her way from England to Tasmania.

It was a sufficient surprise to meet such a vessel in open sea, but Lauterbach was still more surprised to find the ship's company with their things already packed and ready to leave the ship. How was this?

The explanation was given by the captain of the dredger, grinning all over his face. They had heard on their way about the doings of the *Emden*, and also how the *Emden* treated the crews of captured ships. When the dredger's men saw the ship approaching there could not be any doubt that it was the *Emden*, and they therefore packed their possessions and stood by

the railing ready to leave the ship. The further
reports of the captain explained why the crew
seemed so delighted by the capture. This was
the second crew who had had a voyage to
Tasmania in a dredger. The first had gone down
during a severe storm, and the present crew,
including the captain, had demanded their whole
wages in advance as compensation for the danger
of navigating such a small vessel on the high
seas. The voyage had been bad enough, and the
crew had often been threatened with the fate of
the crew of the first dredger. They were therefore thankful at being delivered from the danger
of death by drowning, and expressed without
reserve their gratitude to the *Emden's* ship's
company.

The dredger was hardly clear, when Gaede
opened fire with his guns on the *Ponrabbel*. At
the third shell she turned over with astonishing
speed, and remained floating bottom upwards,
looking like a great whale.

As she had capsized so quickly the air had not
escaped and the dredger would not sink, but a
few more shells helped to give the air an opportunity to escape, and the vessel vanished slowly
beneath the water. Thus the second dredger
from England also went to the bottom. Whether,
in the first years of the war, the English company
would dispatch a third dredger to Tasmania was
extremely doubtful. They must have been tired
of the subject, whereas the crew that was released

from the dredger settled down cheerfully in the *Buresk*, as far as this was possible in the already rather crowded vessel.

Meantime our men had got a lot of necessaries into the boats, which they now brought alongside the *Emden*, emptied, and returned again to the *Clan Grant* for more.

As this unloading went somewhat slowly I was sent over with a few men. When we got to the holds we were overcome. Donnerwetter! What an amount of fine things there were there. We grasped at once that decision was difficult, and time must be wasted. It was necessary, however, to hasten as our Captain did not wish to wait any longer. While we were still stowing the things we needed in the boats the sinking party began their work.

The blasting party first got to work to pierce the bulkheads between the holds and the engine-room, since there were no doors provided. Charges were then laid as deep as possible against the ship's side. Everyone but the sinking and blasting parties left the ship. The English ship's company of the *Clan Grant* were transferred to the *Buresk*. The sea-cocks were opened and the charges fired and, their work done, the parties returned to the *Emden*, and the steam pinnace and the boats were hoisted in.

The *Clan Grant* did not resist for long, but sank slowly down, and finally turned on her side and rolled into the depths.

We now proceeded on an easterly course. This cruise between the evening and the night did not, however, last long, for towards eleven o'clock lights were sighted on the port bow. The *Emden* steamed slowly towards them.

When within hailing distance the ship was ordered by megaphone to stop. Lauterbach was sent over as usual, with his party and Comrade Schall, and soon after came the signal : " English ship *Ben Mohr*, 4,806 tons, with piece goods from England to China and Japan." (72° 55′ E., 8° 16′N.) On the Captain's order that she should be sunk at once the necessary parties went over and commenced their duties.

We were later told that this ship had a valuable cargo, consisting of motors, locomotives, bicycles, various engines, a new and up-to-date motor-boat, etc. The machinery was packed in parts, in cases.

The ship's company of the *Ben Mohr* was sent to the *Buresk*, to Klöpper's great alarm, who did not know where to put these extra men. He therefore requested Lauterbach by megaphone to provide him with mattresses and provisions. In general there seemed to be plenty of provisions laid up in the *Buresk*, for where there was anything to be picked up there was certain to be a party of men from the *Buresk* who had been sent out foraging. This, however, could not be laid to their blame, for with the disproportionate number of men who for want of a proper dump

had to be confined in this ship, considerable
stores were needed. In my opinion they ate well
in the *Buresk*.

After this small incident Lauterbach and the
parties returned to the *Emden*, and soon afterwards the *Ben Mohr* disappeared for ever into
the depths.

In the hope of still further luck we continued
to cruise about thirty sea miles to the westward
of Minicoy.

October 17th passed quietly. Our first officer
divided the booty between the different branches,
during which there were many amusing episodes,
for, as always in such cases, everyone could use
something.

We were proceeding leisurely eastwards. We
passed Minicoy to the south. Next day we were
to turn northwards, as there was nothing more
doing down here.

On October 18th, between midnight and one
in the morning, those not on duty were awakened
by the quicker revolution of the engines, and
hurried on to the upper deck. We saw to starboard a fully-lighted ship, who from her whole
appearance must be a very large mail-packet.
Her speed also favoured this probability.

When we were sufficiently near, this ship was
signalled by Morse, and answered; " Spanish
steamship *Fernando Po*, from Manila to Colombo
and Barcelona."

We thanked her and vanished into the night,

glad not to have been recognised. For safety's sake we proceeded on a fictitious course southwards until the Spaniard had vanished over the horizon, and then turned again to the north.

According to our plans, since nothing was discovered yesterday on the shipping routes, we were to search north-east of Minicoy for victims, as here we would be on the shipping route from Colombo to Bombay.

As this line had not yet been tried by us, we hoped with some certainty that we would find a few ships.

In this neighbourhood we were led by a lucky star. October 18th was a Sunday, and therefore there was first divisions, and then Church was held. After Church the officers off duty gathered as usual in the wardroom for a cocktail or a glass of port, and the Captain also visited us for a chat. In the middle of the conversation it was reported that a smoke cloud was in sight four points on the starboard bow.

We all rushed at once for the bridge and the quarterdeck, and the new arrival was examined through many glasses. It was an hour before part of the ship could be seen on the horizon. The first thing we discovered was a very large funnel, which only said so far that the ship was a merchantman. Soon afterwards, however, a blue streak was to be seen, betraying the fact that this ship was of the Blue Funnel Line, of which we were very glad as this line owns only big ships and we had therefore a very choice morsel before us.

The *Emden* approached her at full speed, and the rest followed swiftly and surely along the usual lines. Lauterbach and von Guerard went over with the prize crew. She was the English steamship *Troilus* of the line mentioned, 7,562 tons, with a cargo of copper, tin, rubber, and other piece goods, from Colombo to England. A valuable capture! The value of the cargo was estimated at a round twenty-five million marks, with the then favourable exchange.

On board this ship were a few passengers, among them one lady who gave rise to an amusing episode. The meeting provided a proof of the smallness of the world.

As usual Lauterbach was the first aboard the English ship, in full " war paint." On the deck the lady suddenly came up to him with the words : " Mr. Lauterbach, how are you ? "

Speechlessness on the part of the prize officer, accompanied by searchings of memory !

With great vivacity the lady explained that she had spent a few days on board the *Staatssekretär Krätke,* a former command of Lauterbach's. Naturally Lauterbach could not remember her, for the big German ship carried a large number of passengers, whom the captain did not especially notice. The Englishwoman must have been impressed or pleased by Lauterbach's martial

appearance, for she recognised him at once. I
cannot say what effect the sharpness of her
memory had on Lauterbach. Like a typical
Englishwoman, this lady was very amused by the
capture of the ship by the *Emden*, and particularly
by Mr. Lauterbach.

Exactly the opposite, anger and contempt, was
the condition of the captain of the *Troilus*. He
had asked the Naval Staff in Colombo on which
route he would be out of danger of the damned
Emden. The Naval Staff advised him to steam
thirty nautical miles north of the usual shipping
route, as that route was absolutely safe. It was
just on this line that he had run right into our
arms.

It was easy to understand his anger against
the Naval Staff, as his ship had only been completed a few months and this was her first
voyage.

What gave most pleasure to us in the *Emden*
about his anger, was that he blurted out the
very useful information for us that the English
held the safest route to be thirty miles north
of the Colombo to Aden route. We could
therefore await more ships with certainty on
this route recommended by the English Naval
Staff.

All our officers rejoiced at the capture of the
Troilus, except the excellent Klöpper, who inquired where in the small and simple *Buresk* he
was to put such a number of seamen, and a lady

in addition who naturally must have a cabin to herself.

In the meantime the *Troilus* was ordered to follow. She would be sunk later. The *Emden* did not wish to lose any time in this favourable locality but to be on with the hunt at once.

The claims on our patience were great, for again we hoped and expected great things, but the whole afternoon passed without any luck, and it was only between eight and nine o'clock that a light was sighted on the port bow. We could not tell, however, with whom we had to deal, for this suspicious ship was steaming without direction lights. The usual alarm was sounded for safety's sake, and, ready and armed for every emergency, the *Emden* approached her new victim. *Buresk* and *Troilus* were ordered to follow us.

Only when we were quite near could the harmlessness of the ship be made out. She was a merchant ship with one funnel, and at once obeyed the Morse signal to stop. (75° 7′ E., 8° 16′ N.) This time Geerdes and Fikentscher went over with the prize crew. An Englishman again, the 5,596 ton steamship, *St. Egbert*, with sugar and piece goods from Colombo to New York.

The ship herself was English, but her cargo was neutral property, and must therefore be respected whether we would or not. The misfortune had, however, one advantage ; the *St. Egbert* could be used as a dump. Klöpper must have been somewhat relieved at this news, for he was having a difficult time in the *Buresk* with the large number of English sailors.

Geerdes was therefore ordered to follow the *Emden* with his prize, owing to the lack of time and the darkness in which nothing could be done.

Steaming in echelon, to starboard the *Buresk* and the *St. Egbert*, and to port the *Troilus*, we proceeded on our previous course, but not for long, for soon after midnight the lights of a steamship were sighted on the port bow.

The *Emden* was after the new vessel at increased speed, with the convoy coming leisurely after. The stranger was soon reached. (75° 7' E., 8° 39' N.)

This time Levetzow and I had the pleasure of the capture. We were rowed over in the lifeboat, and with some curiosity went aboard the ship. Our prize crew was soon posted and Levetzow and I then went to the captain on the bridge, where we were shown the ship's papers.

A pleasant surprise awaited us there. The captured English ship, the *Exford*, 4,542 tons, was loaded with 5,500 tons of the best Cardiff coal. Like the *Buresk* she was chartered for the British Admiralty, and was *en route* for the East. This report was quickly passed on to the *Emden*, for we wished our people to have the good news as soon as possible. I must here emphasise that the captain's behaviour was exemplary; he made our duties easy for us in every way.

Once again we had coal of the best and in plenty. With this supply we could work a whole year.

The *Emden* sent the order: " Follow between *Emden* and *Troilus*."

Levetzow took this order and saw to its execution. I revisited the sentries posted, and gave orders for the extinguishing of all lights, for we had to steam in complete darkness. I then went up to the chart-house and talked to the captain, who was told the fate of his ship and advised to pack up his things and tell his men to do the same.

The night's steaming passed quite quietly for us. The bad functioning of the engine-room telegraph was, however, unpleasant. We had always to be signalling to the men in the engine room that more revolutions were necessary, in order to preserve the requisite distance from the *Emden*.

For a time all went well, but then the old tub began to steam too fast, so that there was a danger of passing the *Emden*. The telegraph was quickly used, but before its effect was visible the *Exford* had too much way. Again the telegraph rang in the engine room and soon the speed was too slow. Thus the *Exford* swung back and forth. It was no easy matter to steam in a large company with a ship with such antiquated equipment. One would think that with such a tub it would be easy, but a clear idea of the conditions can only be gained by practice.

Geerdes in the *St. Egbert* had a greater trial than ours in the *Exford*. In the night there was a tropical rain-squall, in which he lost touch, and found himself alone on the high seas. What was to be done next ?

Geerdes and Fikentscher came to the decision to stop and wait for the day. The English ship's company naturally saw at once what was wrong, but kept quiet. For safety Geerdes placed sentries at all the important points in the ship, so that at least nothing could be laid to his charge which might lead to the loss of the captured ship.

When all was clear he proceeded on his previous course, looking for the *Emden* and her convoy. On October 19th the *Emden* and her train lay to and waited for the *St. Egbert*, who fortunately found her way back to us at seven in the morning.

Already while waiting for the *St. Egbert* the *Emden* got out the steam pinnace, the pinnace, and both life-boats, to take all the captured ships' companies over to the *St. Egbert*, and naturally the Englishmen from the *Buresk* as well.

The plentiful provisions in the *Troilus* were transferred principally to the *Buresk*, where there were many mouths to be filled. This took up a good deal of time, but the quiet sea was in our favour. The difficult task of transferring the men fell to the first officer, Kapitänleutnant v. Mücke, in person. For this purpose he went over to the *Troilus*.

If the *Emden* had then received a surprise visit from an enemy warship, our Captain would have been fairly well caught, for a good part of the *Emden's* officers and men were divided between the captured ships.

I will give a resumé here, so that the reader can imagine the picture. The *Buresk* can be excepted, as she had supernumerary officers and men as ship's company.

Troilus had Lauterbach and Guerard (Adjutant) with about ten men, and in addition Kapitän leutnant v. Mücke. *St. Egbert* had Geerdes (Officer of the after-battery) and Fikentscher and ten men. *Exford* had Levetzow (second Gunnery Officer) and myself (Second torpedo officer, torpedo flat) and ten men. In addition the men must be reckoned who were manning the steam pinnace and the other three boats, about thirty-two men altogether. Therefore there were seven officers and about sixty-two men out of the *Emden*. In the ship were still the Captain, who could not leave the ship, the Gunnery Officer, the Torpedo Officer, and two Lieutenants.

That was the situation with regard to officers and men when towards nine o'clock a smoke cloud came in sight.

The *Emden* quickly hoisted in one cutter and went off at full speed towards the new victim, which came from the direction of Aden.

Owing to the lack of men the new prize crew could only be very small in numbers. The capture was carried out by Leutnant z. S. Zimmermann, with a small prize crew. (75° 4′ E., 9° 22′ N.) This time it was the English ship *Chilkana*, 5,220 tons, of the British India Navigation Co. Her cargo consisted of piece goods and provisions. The ship came from England, and was going to Indian ports. Like the *Troilus*, this ship was quite new and on her first voyage. The *Emden* returned with her to the general halting place.

We in the *Exford* had in the meantime transferred all our Englishmen to the *St. Egbert*. Only the Chinese stokers, who were willing to work for the German flag if they were paid, remained on board. This was most desirable, for we could use our own stokers much better in the *Emden*.

The other ships transferred their ships' companies to the dump, and the Englishmen remaining in the *Buresk* had also gone over. In the course of time this peculiar sea voyage seemed to have become too much for them, though they had followed our activities with much interest.

The most curious piece of luggage belonged to the captain of the *Troilus*. He asked our first officer, v. Mücke, for permission to take his harmonium with him to the *St. Egbert*. Herr v. Mücke gave permission. Unfortunately I could not hear the comments of our men on this piece of furniture removal. This day's activities would have been worth the attention of a cinematograph camera-man.

The *Chilkana* was now also lying beside us, and the transhipment of her ship's company began, for they also had to be transferred to the *St. Egbert*. The provisions in the most recent prize were still more plentiful than those in the *Troilus*, and Kapitän v. Müller therefore gave orders to stop provisioning from the *Troilus* and change over to the *Chilkana*. Kapitänleutnant v. Mücke, accompanied by his staff and Lauterbach, therefore went over to the new provision ship. Three fully-loaded boats of food were shipped to the dump, which was provisioned thoroughly.

Meantime a blasting and sinking party were sent over to the *Troilus*, which was now to be done away with. A careful search of the *Chilkana* revealed that this brand-new ship had a very fine wireless installation. The Adjutant with some of his experts therefore went and dismounted the whole thing, which was transferred to the *Exford*, so that our new collier was now equipped with all the most modern methods of signalling. A good stock of chemicals was also discovered in the *Chilkana*, the removal of which was superintended by the *Emden's* two doctors.

The *Chilkana* was now empty. The freed boats, which had taken the ships' companies to the *St. Egbert*, came alongside the *Chilkana*. The *Buresk* also sent Gyssling with two of her boats. Nobody wished to be behindhand with the provisioning.

The division of the stores was so carried out that the *Emden* and her companion ships each received provisions in proportion to her complement of men. As soon as the boats were full they departed for their destination, were quickly unloaded, returned to the *Chilkana*, and the process was repeated. Drinks, crockery, knives and forks, and linen, of which there was plenty in the *Chilkana*, were also divided between *Emden* and *Buresk*.

A fully-loaded boat presented quite a comic appearance. There were whole hams, sausages, tinned goods of all kinds, sacks of table linen, whole baskets filled with plates, cups, tea and coffee pots, saucepans and frying-pans, knives, forks and spoons. One thought oneself at a great fair. Other boats carried tea, chocolate in all its forms, cases of bottled beer, hundreds of boxes of condensed milk, and many other good things.

On the side that was clear of traffic the *Emden* had meanwhile opened fire on the *Troilus*, as the ship was very well built and would not sink. Several salvoes only made her sink a little deeper. She had apparently no intention of disappearing beneath the water. This arresting spectacle was naturally carefully watched by the people in the *St. Egbert,*and many photographs were taken. With the mass of men in her the latter looked like an emigrant ship.

We in the *Exford* lay close to the *Emden*, and watched the whole spectacle with great enjoyment. A look out had, however, to be kept, for the ships were always in motion with wind and current, and our engines were kept moving.

Levetzow, who was in charge, was once forced to hail the *Emden* : " Please go full speed ahead. My engines do not function astern."

That was the worst of these engines. If the *Emden* had not at once gone full speed ahead, the *Exford* would have had her bows planted in the stern of the *Emden*. Safe navigation of such a tub was impossible. Later these defects were remedied by our engine-room staff.

The *Exford* received no more provisions as she was already well supplied. The *Emden* took some flour over from us, while we received some oil from the *Buresk* in exchange.

Between one and two o'clock the new ship's company came on board the *Exford*. Kapitän-leutnant Gropius, who was navigating officer in the *Emden*, was given the command. His place was filled by Lauterbach. The Germans in the *Exford* were, in addition : Leutnant z. S. Schall, Bootsmann Müller as officers of watches, Maschinist Fischer as chief engineer, one Steuermannsmaat, three Maschinistenmaate, one signalman, three seamen, and four stokers.

When Levetzow had handed to Gropius his powers as temporary captain of the *Exford*, we two and our prize crew returned to the *Emden*, which we reached just in time for a fascinating spectacle.

There were a number of sharks round the ship,

at which Gaede was shooting, using an ordinary
military rifle. Gaede was wearing a white topee,
which suddenly fell overboard and floated shining
on the water, and the largest of the sharks rushed
eagerly for this bright object, probably in the
belief that he had got hold of some dainty morsel.
As the monster raised his head Gaede got in the
shot which killed him, and in his death-agony he
vanished into the depths, followed by his kindred
and friends.

It was now three o'clock in the afternoon, and
still " the unsinkable ship," *Troilus*, would not
disappear from the picture. This was due to the
fact that these new ships, of which *Troilus* was
one, were made especially water-tight. The compartments under the water-line had many more
divisions than the older vessels. The ship, however, had to be sunk, in spite of her newness, and
the *Emden* therefore had to fire more shells in her
endeavour to sink this well-built ship. Only at
six in the evening, a full three hours later, did the
Troilus take her last leave.

Towards four o'clock the unloading of the
Chilkana was finished, after the boats had been
backward and forward at least four or five times.
We had now, however, plenty of provisions on
board and were a correspondingly greater distance
from starvation.

The *Chilkana* was given over to von Mücke and
Zimmermann and their party. The sea-cocks
were opened and the blasting charges fired.

At four-thirty the *Emden* fired a few rounds at the *Chilkana*, whereat this ship went under so quickly that she sunk before the *Troilus*. Soon Geerdes and his men returned from the *St. Egbert*, and reported that according to orders he had conveyed instructions to the captain not to put into Bombay or Colombo, or any Indian port. The captain was told that if he was encountered on forbidden ways all guarantees would be abrogated, and his ship would be sunk without mercy.

There was great surprise at this report. Our Captain's orders must have been misunderstood, in so far as the captain of the *St. Egbert* had been forbidden to put in at any harbour in India.

According to Geerdes the captain, who had not taken the order too tragically, had returned hearty thanks for good treatment and particularly for the fact that his ship had been spared.

No thanks were due to us for this, but to the fact that he was carrying a neutral cargo. The effect of the misunderstood orders was not serious, but it crossed the plans of our Captain, who had wished that the *St. Egbert* with her 5–600 men on board should put in at some small Indian port and thus create unrest among the native population.

As the *St. Egbert* had already steamed away it was impossible to correct the mistake. Towards half-past six the *Emden* with all her boats hoisted in again, and followed by the *Buresk* and the *Exford*, made after the *St. Egbert*, which was now given correct orders. She then altered course for

Cochin, where, as we later heard, she arrived safely with her living cargo.

We took a fictitious course, but this time in a special way. At first our course was southerly, but while still within sight of the *St. Egbert* we turned northwards. After nightfall we finally took up our correct course southwards.

CHAPTER X

FOR this night all captures were renounced. The look out did sight the lights of a ship at about one in the morning, but no notice was taken. The *Emden's* men had to rest after the strain of the last few days, and it was the Captain's intention with the slow-moving *Exford* to get as far from the shipping routes as possible. In addition the *Emden's* new cruise must not be discovered, for the Captain's plan was to reach Penang unseen and effect a surprise there.

About two o'clock another ship was sighted, unlighted with the exception of the side lights, going past us at very great speed. On account of her speed a guess was hazarded that she was a warship. In fact we found out later that the English auxiliary-cruiser, *Empress of Russia*, was cruising in this locality at that time.

At about three o'clock another ship passed astern of us. We could not make out whether she was a merchant-ship or another auxiliary-cruiser. The funny part of the whole thing was that we were not sighted, which amply proves the efficiency of our dousing arrangements.

During this eventful night we lost the

Buresk, which, however, was soon afterwards found again.

On October 20th we kept to a southerly course, south of the shipping routes from Aden to Colombo, where we were to turn east.

The day was claimed principally by the first officer for the division of yesterday's booty, which made a gay scene on the deck of the *Emden*. Kapitänleutnant v. Mücke was enthroned amidst the fine things which he divided between the various messes. During the process it became clear that we had too much of some things and too little of others, but next day was to bring a remedy for this.

On October 21st in the forenoon the *Emden* stopped, and Haas went over to the *Exford* to look at the engines and boilers, which needed a thorough refit. The opportunity was seized by v. Mücke for an exchange of provisions with the *Exford*. The provisioning two days before had been done so quickly that it had been impossible to make a proper distribution.

As *Exford* was to be detached, to meet us at a prearranged point, an exchange of personnel was also undertaken. Schall and Signalman Lindner returned to the *Emden*. Nautical instruments and charts were sent over. Instructions were sent with them to remain at the rendezvous till lack of provisions forced them to run for a neutral port. The *Exford* left us towards evening.

October 22nd.   Birthday of the Kaiserin !

In honour of Her Majesty, in addition to the
saluting of the colours, which took place every day
at eight o'clock, the mast-head flags were also flown.
At ten o'clock there were divisions in Sunday
dress, and an address by the Captain. Kapitän
v. Müller spoke briefly of the anniversary and
recalled the activity of the Kaiserin in welfare
work and hospital work by which Her Majesty
had shown herself an exemplary mother of her
country. She was to be remembered with gratitude to-day, for during the war she would be
specially active in bringing gentleness and good
to the Fatherland. This gratitude should be expressed in true seaman's fashion in three cheers,
given from good German hearts. We joined in
heartily. The orchestra played the national
anthem. It was very ceremonious and stirring.

Towards noon we altered course to east. In
honour of the day there was a specially good midday meal. Among us in the wardroom v. Mücke
remembered the Kaiserin with a few heart-felt
words.

In the course of the day we arrived in the
southern part of the Bay of Bengal, but stood
to southward of the shipping route from Colombo
to Singapore. There was therefore no activity
against the enemy, and the men deserved their
rest, for the efforts of the past weeks required a
break.

The following day also brought no new ships,

and this desirable quiet time was occupied with the necessary military exercises, particularly fighting exercises. These had to be carried out, for there was certainly every prospect of a fight in Pulo-Penang Harbour, where there were certain to be enemy warships lying. As we had had no action evolutions for a long time, the men had this time to be made thoroughly familiar with their action stations. After a few exercises our gallant men were so perfect in their duties that all went well, and with even brilliant smoothness.

As well as these evolutions the gunlayers, gunnery specialists, and range-finders were given an opportunity for still further practice. The *Buresk* towed a target, on which we held both firing and range-finding practice.

Our next objective was the Nicobar Islands, where the *Emden* was to coal again to as large an extent as possible, for no one knew when there would be another opportunity.

On October 26th these islands came in sight, and at seven we ran into Nancowrie Harbour. The *Buresk* anchored first and the *Emden* went alongside her and made fast.

Coaling was begun soon afterwards, and the men worked marvellously, reaching an average of 69 tons an hour. By about four o'clock the necessary 500 tons had been taken in. In consideration of the coming fight coal was not stored on deck, for if scattered by a shell falling on the deck would have too easily reached the guns' crews, so that it would be more danger than use.

Our ship was now lying in a bay which was perfectly beautiful. Nancowrie Harbour lies on the south side of the island of Nicobar, and possesses fine, luxuriant, tropical vegetation, which was refreshing to look at after the long sea voyage.

During our stay the *Buresk* was robbed of her name and the name of her port, so that she should not at once be recognised. Her captain, Klöpper, was instructed to steam to a rendezvous west of the island of Sumatra, and to wait there for the *Emden* as long as her provisions should hold out. The instructions were similar to those given to Captain Gropius of the collier *Exford.*

At half-past four we cast off, and the *Buresk* weighed anchor and put to sea. The *Emden* followed and started for Penang at a speed of twelve knots.

Slowly the *Buresk* vanished on the horizon.

During the evening we cruised on the shipping route from Calcutta to Singapore, but could not sight a ship. We had no intention of taking any ship, and would have avoided any we sighted, as the *Emden* had to get to Penang unseen and make an effective surprise.

The night passed without disturbance.

On October 27th speed was increased early in

the morning to 15 knots. In the forenoon there
was a meeting for all officers and the Captain,
who made known to us in detail his plans for the
next day. Each officer had exact instructions
for every emergency, for we had to reckon on the
disabling of every officer, and even of the Captain
himself.

In the meantime the men had cleared the ship
for action, and many things that might have
hindered were stowed away. A larger amount
of ammunition was placed ready at the guns, etc.
We also had a thorough " clean ship," of which
the *Emden* stood in great need. In the afternoon
the men were given a change of clothes and there
were baths. Everyone was to go into the fight
as clean as possible.

At five the order was passed : " Everybody
aft ! "

The Captain briefly told the men what was
intended for to-morrow, and in conclusion he
expressed the hope that everyone would do his
duty faithfully.

The enthusiasm of our brave men could be seen
in their eyes. Thank God we were able to trust
the whole ship's company thoroughly, and so it
had to be for the tasks to be accomplished and
which were carried out.

The first wish of everyone in the *Emden* had
always been to come up against an enemy warship.
The sinking of merchantmen was quite all right,
but it was no deed of arms for a man to be properly

proud of. A fight with similar weapons gave everybody satisfaction, as a trial of the fitness of the ship, her officers and men. This ardent wish was to be granted, and was the cause of the joy and enthusiasm of our men.

If an officer asked his men : " Now ! Are you glad about to-morrow ? " the answer came at once : " Surely, for now we shall get to grips with the real enemy."

Many readers may perhaps ask why we had not long ago set out to look for enemy warships.

To this I would give the only answer, that this is not the proper duty of a cruiser on foreign station. Our orders were quite definite to destroy the enemy's trade. To carry out this duty as completely as possible the *Emden* had to remain as long as possible unassailed, and this could only be achieved by avoiding a fight with enemy warships as far as possible.

It may be asked why we now sought a fight, and went into the lion's den to get it. The answer to this question is also simple and easy to give. We had in the last weeks done an enormous amount of harm to enemy trade, which was severely felt. We had therefore fulfilled the greater part of our duty. The danger of being quickly and completely wiped out in Penang was not too great, as our principal weapon was attack. The maxim which says that " attack is the best defence " was valid for us.

PRINCE FRANCIS JOSEPH OF HOHENZOLLERN

We reckoned, with at least 90 per cent. of certainty, that we should be able to deal with the enemy before we were really noticed. Naturally in this enterprise our fourth funnel was to play a great part in the deception of the enemy by changing the appearance of the *Emden*. Also we hoped to be able to destroy the other shipping anchored in Pulo-Penang.

Our plan was therefore favourable, and our hope great. Success would bring a double victory, physical and moral.

Towards eight in the evening speed was increased to 17 knots. We wished to reach our objective by dawn. In darkness it would have been impossible, for the entrance to Penang is so narrow and without light one is liable to go ashore. It was further to be assumed that vigilance would diminish at dawn, for the sharper it is by night the more certain is this diminution.

To give the reader a clear picture, a description of Penang and its harbour is briefly given, and an opinion may be formed of the boldness necessary to attack such a harbour.

Coming out of the Straits of Molucca from the west or the north-west one must pass through a channel perhaps a thousand yards broad, between the island of Pulo-Penang on the west and the sandy coast of the peninsula of Molucca. In order to enter the harbour the ship is forced

to round the north side of Pulo-Penang with
helm hard a-starboard, great care being taken
not to run too far to port owing to the danger of
running aground on the flat shore. When safely
round this corner the mouth of the harbour is
visible, a kind of bottle-neck. There is indeed
an opening to the south, but this can only be
used by shallow-draught ships.

On the island itself, inside the bay, is the town
of Georgetown, with the harbour buildings. On
the north side stands an old fort, which we had
not to reckon with as it was of completely obsolete
construction.

We must now imagine an enemy warship entering the harbour, engaging the anchored warships,
and having, in order to leave again, to turn in the
narrow space of the harbour. Through our own
activities against merchant shipping we had to
reckon with the fact that there would certainly
be a large number of merchant-ships lying in the
harbour, which would still further limit the space
for turning. If, as was easily possible, there was
a torpedo-boat lying in some corner, it would be
easy for her during the fight to creep unseen far
enough towards the *Emden* to get in a fatal shot
with a torpedo. It would be impossible to get
clear, even if we succeeded in sighting the torpedo-
boat in time.

The dangers of our attack were therefore many
and great. Success could only be gained by cold-
blooded consideration followed by remorseless

execution. Second thoughts and hesitations were useless.

In the *Emden* there was not a moment's doubt as to our victory, for we knew the fine character and capabilities of our Captain. He was the very man to lead his ship to success in such a perilous venture.

In the plan of attack at least one torpedo played a part, for our enemy was to be sunk by a torpedo from the *Emden* before he should properly have had time to think about resistance.

Up to midnight we had light war watches, but from midnight onwards full war watches were set.

Towards two o'clock the light of Pulo-Penang came in sight. Everyone in the *Emden* was roused. After washing there was a good break-fast with milk soup, so that everyone should be fit for the fighting. When the watches were changed those coming off duty also washed and fed.

Our fourth funnel was already hoisted, and looked quite imposing, rising from the deck.

Soon after the sighting of the light, we sighted the lights of a steamship entering the harbour. The moon was still shining clearly, and increased the danger that we would be sighted by the signal station which was situated on a height. The *Emden* therefore turned, and cruised until the moon went down.

We turned about, approached at eleven knots,

and quickly and boldly turned towards the mouth
of the harbour.   This part of the proceedings was
greatly helped by the brightly burning light-buoy,
at whose bright light we were much astonished.
Soon we passed the ship we had already sighted,
which was now probably waiting for the pilot.
At half-past four in the morning came the order :
" Ready ! "   We passed a small island lying in
front of the harbour, especially suitable for cover
for guard-boats.   Later we sighted a few fishing-
boats whose crews kept such a poor look-out that
we nearly ran one of them down.

We scarcely had the island behind us when a
pilot-boat approached us to within twenty yards.
What the pilot made of our appearance I do not
know, but he was hardly likely to have taken us
for an enemy warship.

At 4.50 a.m. we entered the bottle-neck and
again received the order :   " Ready ! "   We all
rushed for our action-stations, I for the torpedo
flat, where I went over all the arrangements
again.   The torpedo tubes were already loaded
and the electric release-gear connected up.   It
was ready for firing.

Naturally the communication with the conning-
tower had been joined up, and the order to
" clear ship " obeyed here as elsewhere.   This communication served principally for the transmission
of news from above.   In the torpedo flat we could
see nothing, and naturally wished to be kept in
touch with the progress of the attack.   At

5.5 a.m. we received the order from above : " Clear away starboard tube." We waited with suspense for the order to release the torpedo.

At 5.18 a.m. there appeared on the torpedo flat telegraph the illuminated word " Fire ! "

The torpedo was out and away. There followed some seconds of suspense and breathless listening. There was a dull report.

There were cheers and general congratulations in the flat. There was no doubt that the torpedo had got home and therefore done its work.

Simultaneously with the report the guns opened fire above. In our enclosed flat the noise of the salvoes was considerable. Unfortunately we could see nothing.

Then came the news from the conning-tower, " Torpedo got home, well under the water-line, but has not completely dealt with the Russian cruiser *Jemtschug* "—this was the ship—" and another torpedo is therefore to be fired."

We quickly reloaded the starboard tube and immediately after came the order: " Clear away port tube." The electrical release-gear was connected up, and we waited for the order to fire.

The *Emden* canted to one side, from which we inferred that she was turning.

The electric signals showed : " Ready ! "

We signalled back : " Everything ready ! "

Shortly afterwards followed the order : " Fire ! "

The torpedo rushed hissing out of the tube. At

once there was a fearful crash which also gave the *Emden* a considerable shock.

Rejoicing in the submerged flat ! We greeted the noise and the shock as a proof that this shot had got home, probably in the magazine or torpedo flat of the Russian, as the tremendous explosion was not otherwise explicable.

We soon received news from the conning-tower that the Russian had vanished, with the addition : " We are leaving the harbour."

Now that my presence was no longer necessary in the flat, I rushed for the deck to see what remained of the proceedings.

A cloud of yellow smoke rolled over the place where the *Jemtschug* had lately been. Of the Russian cruiser only the tops of the masts and some floating fragments were to be seen.

Soon afterwards I found my good friend and comrade v. Levetzow, who told me the whole proceedings as they had appeared from the upper deck. I insert the description here, so that the reader may have a proper picture of the fight.

Levetzow's description begins at the point at which I had had to go below to the torpedo flat. Dawn was beginning (4.50 a.m.) and the coast, to port the mainland, and to starboard the island of Pulo-Penang, could already be clearly recognised. Georgetown was still brightly lighted, which circumstance greatly assisted our approach. The guiding-buoys were taken for exact bearings.

Before entering the harbour we reduced speed.
To starboard we saw four lights, which gave the
impression that we had to do with torpedo-boats,
but we soon recognised our mistake. It was a
warship with several masts and funnels. The
day broke. The *Emden* had her mast-head flags
proudly flying. The enemy warship was now
recognised. She was the Russian light-cruiser
Jemtschug, of about the build and power of the
Emden, and therefore a worthy enemy.

The first torpedo officer, Oberleutnant z. S.
Witthoeft, hurried at once into the conning-tower
and gave the orders for clearing away the torpedo
tubes. The *Emden* went so close to the Russian
that the torpedo could not miss. At 380 yards
we fired, and the torpedo hastened to its goal.
Exactly at 5.18 there was a muffled report, and
the Russian rose for a moment and then sank
back up to her deck at the stern. At the same
time the *Emden's* starboard guns opened fire with
a frightful crash. Their objective was the forecastle of the *Jemtschug*, in which were the men's
flats. The object was to put the men out of
action before they could reach their guns.

It was a fearful sight. In a short time the
fore part of the ship was in flames. The ship's
side was pierced like a sieve, and glowing with
the great heat. It was indeed an awful and
enthralling sight.

Soon after the first torpedo had been fired the
Emden turned sharply to port, as there was

considerable danger of running into the many merchant-ships that were anchored close to us.

Shortly after the torpedo-officer in the conning-tower, who was also the officer for fighting tactics, gave the order : " Clear away port tube ! Load starboard tube ! " A second torpedo was to be fired, to deal completely with the Russian and prevent her firing a torpedo at us. On the inquiry of the Torpedo-Officer as to whether the port torpedo might be fired, the Captain's consent was given.

Suddenly a few shells from an unknown direction passed over our heads. Some of these came from the *Jemtschug*, where a few gallant men had manned the after guns and returned our fire. Some of the Russians preferred to jump into the water and swim for safety to the shore. The majority of the shells, however, came from the interior of the harbour. The miscreant was soon discovered. It was the French destroyer *d'Iberville*, who had not the courage to show herself. We would be on her back as soon as we had fired our second torpedo.

Our ship was not hit by the shells. The sufferer was a Japanese ship, who received one or two of the shells which had gone too high in her funnel.

Meanwhile the *Emden* had come up to within 700 yards of the crippled Russian. Our guns raked the whole deck of the *Jemtschug*, whose fire was forced to cease.

Torpedo-Officer Witthoeft pressed the electric

button for the port tube. The torpedo leapt hissing out of the tube and rushed unerringly towards the enemy. A few seconds later there was a frightful report, and the Russian cruiser was literally torn into two parts. Huge pieces of metal flew about in the air and fell back noisily into the water. The spectacle only lasted for a few seconds, when a thick cloud of yellow smoke hid the scene of destruction, looking like a mountain spouting fire, with green and yellowish flames darting out from it, followed by detonations. It was a wonderful and awful spectacle.

After three, or perhaps four, minutes the veil of smoke rose, but except for the tops of the masts rising out of the water there was nothing to be seen of the *Jemtschug*.

The whole affair only took about fifteen minutes. The *Emden* intended to wheel and make an end of the destroyer *d'Iberville*, when a vessel appeared in the entrance to the harbour surrounded by a cloud of thick smoke. In the belief that this ship was a torpedo-boat the *Emden* turned quickly to port and went at full speed towards the entrance to the harbour, towards the new enemy.

So far the report of my friend, v. Levetzow.

We watched the new enemy from the quarter-deck. The irritating smoke clouds hindered us from recognising her. As the mysterious darkness would not clear away we opened fire at about 6,000 yards. In consequence of the bad mirage that morning our shooting was not good, but we were thankful when the supposed torpedo-boat turned and disclosed the small and harmless government-boat. Naturally the order to cease fire was given at once.

Insignificant as the little ship was, she had by her appearance saved a number of ships and the *d'Iberville* from destruction. Our Captain had intended to destroy the *d'Iberville* and sink the numerous merchant-ships in the harbour. Now, however, that the *Emden* was outside the harbour the Captain did not wish to enter again.

The mast-head flags were hauled down and the men released from their action stations.

Somewhat later Kapitänleutnant v. Mücke assembled all the men aft and explained to them the progress of the fight. This was worth doing, because a number of the men had action stations under the armoured deck and had therefore seen nothing. The men expressed great pleasure at the *Emden's* success. Finally Kapitän v. Müller gave a short speech in which he said that in view of our success it behoved us to remember the War Lord, and renew our loyalty to him by giving three cheers for His Majesty our most gracious Kaiser !

We gave them with enthusiasm and joy. We were uplifted and refreshed by the thought that something had been accomplished to the greater glory of the Fatherland.

The men were then released, for breakfast

and then to wash. Finally the guns were to be
cleaned, new ammunition was to be placed ready,
and the searchlights were to be made fast.

It may have been seven o'clock, and the men
had already vanished from the waist, when the
order " Clear ship for Action!" was given. We
all rushed for our action stations.

What had happened ?

An apparently very large ship whose flag could
not be recognised from the foretop had appeared
on the horizon. The range was found and passed
to the guns, and the ship turned slightly, so that
we could join action with the whole port side.
Everyone waited for the order to open fire.

This order, however, never came.

At the outset everyone on the bridge had agreed
that the stranger looked like a big auxiliary-
cruiser. The nearer we came, however, the smaller
became the ship, which finally shrank into a quite
ordinary merchantman. She was flying the yellow
flag to show that she had powder on board.

It was the second trick that day the mirage had
played the *Emden*, but no harm was done.

There was no reason to respect the powder ship,
and we therefore proceeded according to the old
receipt to stop her, and Lauterbach and the prize
crew went over. The order to sink the ship was
accompanied by a message, which the captain
was to pass on at the first opportunity. The
Emden had not saved any survivors of the Russian
cruiser *Jemtschug* as there had been plenty of

boats in the vicinity. The government-boat had been fired on under the misapprehension that the *Emden* had to deal with a torpedo-boat. The Captain of the *Emden* therefore wished to express his regrets for these facts.

Of such a noble temperament was our Kapitän v. Müller that he excused himself for mistake and misapprehension. I think that if the case had been reversed we might have had to wait a long time for an apology.

In the "powder chest" Lauterbach had just carried out his errand and posted his men when he was signalled to by the *Emden* to return at once.

The reason was that a very suspicious vessel had been sighted to starboard, which in spite of the distortion due to refraction was certainly a warship. About her size we in the *Emden* could not yet be certain.

Lauterbach at once returned with his cutter, which was hoisted in with all speed. We had to be clear for action as quickly as possible. The now freed powder ship was the English steamship *Glanturret.*

When, on the order "Clear ship for Action," everyone had run for their action stations, I had also rushed down to the torpedo flat. There I at once received from the conning-tower the news that the approaching warship was a French destroyer, and as the torpedo weapons would not be used against so small a ship I could return to the deck.

With mast-head flags flying the *Emden* steamed at high speed towards the new enemy. At 4,700 yards our first salvo was fired. By turning to port the whole starboard side was brought into action.

Our little enemy did not act judiciously. She did not, as would have been correct for a torpedo-boat, come straight towards us. After the first salvo she turned and fled, presenting us with a splendid target of her whole side.

Our first salvo was somewhat high, and the second fell short, but the third got home and could not have gone more exactly according to the prescribed evolutions. The first effective salvo shot down the tricolour and found the boiler-room, for huge white clouds of steam were streaming from the ship.

In spite of severe disablement the enemy did not remain quiet, but fired a torpedo which passed several hundred yards astern of us. Also one gun, which stood forward of the conning-tower, was brought into action. It must have been a machine-gun, for it fired with immense speed, but hit nothing. Most of the shots went over us, and the noise they made was like a swarm of bees.

Our guns shot splendidly. After we had found the range every round told.

The enemy was in a bad condition. Her super-structure was all shot to pieces, and everything else as well.

After the *Emden's* twelfth salvo the Frenchman

disappeared in a cloud of yellowish smoke. Our Captain therefore ordered the "cease fire."

When the cloud cleared away the torpedo-boat was still afloat, but gave no sign of being willing to surrender.

The *Emden* therefore opened fire again and fired another ten salvoes, with the effect that the Frenchman would never be able to move from the spot. The order was given : " Battery cease fire ! " and the *Emden* came up so that she came to a standstill a little aft of the torpedo-boat to avoid a possible torpedo.

Meanwhile the Frenchman had plunged bows forward, and gradually sank deeper till, with her bows apparently on the bottom, she stood upright in the water, with her stern high above the surface. This did not, however, last long, and the stern also vanished into the deep.

Except wreckage and swimming survivors there was nothing more to be seen.

The *Emden* came up to about 200 yards from the place where she had sunk. While the mast-head flags were being lowered our second cutter was lowered into the water, with an officer, and the assistant doctor with bandages, etc., in addition to her usual complement. Soon afterwards the first cutter followed with an officer. She had been made properly fast for the fight, and had to be cast off, which naturally took some time.

With all speed we joined in the work of rescue,

which we naturally thought to be easy and straight-forward. We had made a mistake, however, for the unwounded Frenchmen would not let themselves be rescued or taken out of the water.

The reason for such a mad refusal remains a mystery to me. Probably the men had been told such bogy stories of the Germans that they would rather risk their lives in trying to swim to the neighbouring coast than fall into the hands of the " man-eating barbarians." One of these Frenchmen did indeed, we heard later, reach Pulo-Penang Island, a quite good task for a swimmer.

When the French seamen saw with what care the wounded were hoisted into the boats they gained confidence rapidly, so that altogether we were able to save thirty-six men and one lieutenant.

With this cargo of men the cutters came alongside the *Emden*. The wounded at first remained in the boats. Those unwounded came in over the boom.

As it was necessary to get the wounded on board without too much pain the boats were hoisted amidships. Here the Frenchmen were carefully lifted out and taken at once into our sick-berth, which is in the fore part of the ship, in compartments XI and XII, and placed in the berths. The poor fellows, who had fought well for their country, were a pitiful sight. Three men in particular were very bad. One of them I have always before my eyes when I think of his pain. The poor fellow had been hit in the stomach, so that all his entrails were hanging out.

It was unfortunate that the wounded had been some time in the sea water, as it quickly aggravated the wounds.

Our doctors went to work straight away. Two of the wounded had had their legs shot away, so that these limbs had at once to be amputated. The wounds were already festering, which made the doctors' work more difficult.

The unwounded were accommodated in the starboard waist, which made tolerable lodging with the help of a breadth of tent cloth, and was certainly more agreeable than between decks near the engines where it was suffocatingly hot. In any case we had no room between decks for prisoners.

To guard the sound Frenchmen sentries were placed, who also stopped them swarming over the *Emden* which naturally interested them. From them we learnt that the destroyer we had sunk bore the name of *Mousquet*. This was confirmed by a life-buoy which one of our cutter's crew had fished out and brought on board. This single trophy was proudly hung on the quarter-deck.

In consequence of their good handling the Frenchmen were communicative. They told us their movements of the previous night, some parts of which were very interesting to us.

Mousquet had been on patrol duty at the north

entrance to Penang Harbour, and her head-
quarters had been in the neighbourhood of the
island which we had passed in the morning. The
men said that they had seen a cruiser going in
but had been misled by our fourth funnel.
They were convinced that they had to do with an
English cruiser.

We were not quite clear about the behaviour
of the Frenchmen. If the *Mousquet* was lying in
wait behind the island they were either not keeping
a look out or had neglected their duty in not
hailing the ship entering (us), and reporting us
in the harbour. Only by hailing her could the
officer on duty in the *Mousquet* be certain about
the incoming ship.

Upon the report of our torpedo—so said the
Frenchmen—they had hurried into the harbour
to find out what was happening. In entering
they encountered us, but again they had been
silent, taking us for an Englishman.

And so it was also in the open sea, for otherwise
the *Mousquet* would certainly not have confidently
and quietly run towards the German enemy.
The Frenchmen were first brought to their senses
by the gunfire of the *Emden*. The shock of this
awakening to the captain had robbed him of his
senses, and made him stupid enough to seek
safety in flight, and thus expose the side of his
vessel to our gunfire instead of coming towards
us.

Asked about the proceedings in the *Mousquet*,

the Frenchmen said that part of the ship's company had put up a stout resistance. Another part of the crew were hurled overboard, and this was mistaken by others who voluntarily threw themselves into the water.

Confused as the French captain had been by the realisation that he had been betrayed into a fight with the *Emden*, he remained courageous up to his last breath. In the course of the fight his legs were shot away, but he had wished to remain standing on the bridge till the end of the fight, so had himself lashed to the bridge. The captain went down with his ship—a hero's death for his fatherland !

Most of the Frenchmen saved only their lives, and they were therefore given new underclothes and uniforms out of the *Emden's* store. The prisoners were treated as well as possible. The behaviour of the *Emden's* ship's company was even touching, for in the goodness of their hearts they brought the Frenchmen chocolate, cigarettes, and many refreshing drinks. It could be seen in the faces of the prisoners that they were grateful and content with the change in their fortunes.

The French sub-lieutenant was severely wounded and was given a special room in the sick-ward. After an operation—he had to have his right foot amputated—I paid him a visit. He was fairly contented, but complained of frightful pain. I told him how many of his men had been saved and what had befallen himself, and this quieted him. He was also very grateful that he did not have to worry about his fellow-prisoners.

Many items of news were gathered from the Frenchmen—for example, the news that only Japanese ships were lying in the harbour of Singapore. We gathered from this that the English must have sent their ships home.

It was news for us that on October 14th the English cruiser *Yarmouth* had brought in to Singapore the *Pontoporos*, which we had abandoned. It was probable that our faithful companion the *Markomannia* had been sunk by her own ship's company, since at that time she must have been lying with the *Pontoporos* off Simalur.

Conversation between the *Emden's* men and the Frenchmen was limited, as our men would certainly report any news of importance. In this way it came to light that the French officers had told their men that the Germans killed all their prisoners. For this reason the Frenchmen did not want to be rescued, and therefore some tried to reach the land by swimming. So their joy was much greater at the good treatment they received in the *Emden*. What we had previously guessed was confirmed by the Frenchmen.

I must confess that I do not understand the policy of saying nothing but bad of your enemy. If, in consequence, men are drowned, the responsibility rests solely on the French authorities. Perhaps, however, they believed the men would fight better under such circumstances, but this would be a poor testimony for the spirit of the French navy. I will assume, in honour of our enemies of 1914, that this is not correct.

In the meantime a new opponent had appeared at the entrance to the harbour of Pulo-Penang, but the ship kept a good distance from us. She was the *Fronde*, a sister ship of the *Mousquet*, and had been anchored in the harbour.

What good spirit had protected us?

If we had approached the *d'Iberville* this destroyer could easily have cut off our exit, and our destruction would have been as good as certain.

We now endeavoured to get away, steaming at twenty-two knots in a northerly direction. Certainly this was to run away from the *Fronde* and was an undoubted retreat, but we had good grounds for it, for we knew from wireless messages which we had intercepted that the wireless station at Penang had already broadcasted the information: "*Emden* at Penang!" Descriptions of our exploits were added, naturally in the most modest manner.

It was certain that these announcements would bring around us all our enemies who were in the neighbourhood. Many hounds are sure death to the hare. The *Emden's* best course was to flee from her many enemies, and that was the reason of the high speed we were steaming.

At half-past ten in the forenoon our · wireless picked up more messages, the answers of enemy warships, which confirmed the report concerning the presence of the *Emden* at Penang.

The position of the enemy warships we naturally could not know, but we could roughly estimate their distance from the resistances.

It was sufficient. By rapid steaming we had got a good start and the warships could not catch us easily.

It was the *Fronde*, however, which obstinately insisted in following us, always keeping a prudent distance, and mouthing like some kind of old slut. With astonishing fierceness she shrieked to the world that the " fearful " *Emden*, which had so terribly " assassinated " her sister *Mousquet*, was before her. She continually gave our course and speed, in the eager hope that some ship of the Entente would give chase. The messages intercepted by our wireless showed she was denouncing us wildly. She could not be silenced with our guns, but the fact that the electrical power of our wireless was much stronger and more effective than hers gave us a chance of confusing her messages almost to the point of obliteration. The denunciations of the *Fronde* were considerably disturbed, for our wireless was very powerful and was used industriously.

In addition, we could reckon on the time when the *Fronde* would get " out of breath," that is, her fuel would run out. With her small provision of coal the little ship could not keep up a long chase.

14

The *Emden* besides delighted her gossipy follower with a certain amount of low cunning, for we steamed on a fictitious course, west-north-west. The God of the weather also favoured us rather than the French, and sent a violent rain squall, completely blinding the *Fronde*. Under cover of this squall the *Emden* at once turned north-north-west.

When the sun returned after a good quarter of an hour the horizon was clear again, and nothing was to be seen of the *Fronde*. We tried to discover some trace of her, but the best eyes and the sharpest glasses could find nothing. We had got clear of the Frenchman.

Now we could look back undisturbed at the last few hours, and rejoice at our success.

How much the *Emden* had done. And what luck had accompanied our enterprise. We had been able to make the difficult passage into Penang harbour, and completely destroy an enemy cruiser. Three times we had been fired on without suffering the least damage. For this we were a little sorry, as the *Emden* could have afforded some slight honourable memento. As a conclusion to " this crowded hour," we had been successful in sinking an enemy destroyer. It was a victory indeed, and must have a good moral effect. Every man in the *Emden* looked back on that day with a feeling of gratitude.

In the torpedo branch we were naturally particularly proud, as we had delivered the

stroke responsible for the destruction of the
Jemtschug. Without the effective working of the
two torpedoes the *Emden* would not have achieved
so quickly her decisive results.

In spite of our good fortune, what rather
rankled was that we had not been able to sink
the many ships lying in Penang harbour. There
must have been many a big ship amongst them
that would have made a good figure at the bottom
of the sea.

CHAPTER XI

OUR next objective was the shipping route from Penang to Rangoon. We hoped to surprise some ship to whom we could hand over our prisoners for transport to some neutral port. Speed was reduced, when thanks to the squall we had escaped from the *Fronde*, to seventeen knots.

Till four o'clock we remained on our course, but as no ship would show herself on this line we turned to port and went west-south-west. The *Emden* was to be in the neighbourhood of the Nicobar Islands, which were already known to us, by evening. We were to pass during darkness the St. George Channel, some way to the northward of Nancowrie Harbour, where we had coaled before the attack on Penang.

At about six in the evening the islands came in sight, and it was not long before the *Emden* found herself in the middle of the St. George Channel, which is formed by the two islands of Great and Little Nicobar. The straits, bordered by wooded heights, presented a splendid appearance. After the strain of the day we enjoyed the beautiful scene twice as much. Our Frenchmen, however, showed great anxiety and their behaviour changed so that we inquired into the reason of it. The explanation was that they were afraid that they were to be landed on one of these lonely islands and left to their fate. They were quickly reassured when we told them that such a thought had not occurred to us. We were greatly surprised at the existence of such a fear. I believe that if the case had been reversed such a possibility would have been probable.

At eight in the evening we had the beautiful channel behind us, and the *Emden* turned to port on a south-westerly course. Owing to something being out of order the port engines were running a little hot, so these had to be stopped for the night.

In the night of October 28th two of the wounded Frenchmen died of their wounds. When this was reported to the Captain he gave the order that a ceremonial burial of the bodies was to take place at eight next morning, with full naval honours, for these Frenchmen had died after fighting well for their fatherland.

The burial had to take place quickly because in these tropical regions decay sets in with astonishing rapidity, and in the interest of the health of the ship's company it would not be possible to keep them on board for long.

On October 29th, at eight in the morning, our men were ordered to " fall-in " in parade dress, the officers wearing ordinary service dress and their orders. The unwounded Frenchmen were placed in the starboard waist. Our comrade, Leutnant z. S. Schall, was on the quarter-deck with the guard of honour who were to fire the final salute.

The two bodies, wrapped in sail-cloth and covered with the French tricolour, were placed on the starboard boom, and our men assembled round in a circle. The Captain made a short speech in German and then in French, in which he spoke of the fallen heroes. In conclusion, the Lord's Prayer was repeated.

The *Emden* then stopped, and when both engines were still the bodies were sunk in the sea. Three salvoes were fired over the seamen's grave.

The ship's company dispersed with solemn faces, the engines took up their work, and the voyage proceeded.

The rest of the day was devoted to ordinary duties. The preparations for the fight at Penang were cleared away and the awnings replaced, to allow the men to sleep under cover in the fresh air. The heat in these regions, always very great, is particularly felt in warships, which, owing to their iron construction, form very good conductors. The splendid weather increased the good temper of all on board.

Our French prisoners were content with their lot as far as the continuance of their good treatment. Our men were really touching in their friendliness. They brought the Frenchmen cigarettes, chocolate, and other small things such as can make life tolerable. The wounded Frenchmen were the subject of much anxiety. Although the two doctors of the *Emden* took every trouble to have everything as good as possible for them, the space was insufficient, and the air in the sickward was very close for the wounded men. The sole surviving officer had had a leg amputated and suffered severely. His pain was eased as far as possible.

Our dearest wish was to surprise a ship as soon as possible so that the wounded and the prisoners might be transferred, and the wounded conveyed to a land hospital for better treatment.

In the night of October 29th, however, one of the severely wounded Frenchmen died. All the efforts of our two doctors to save him were in vain.

On October 30th, towards half-past six in the morning, a smoke cloud came in sight, and the *Emden* gave chase. The stranger was a good-sized ship, which relieved our anxiety about our prisoners. Lauterbach went over with the prize crew. She was the English ship *Newburn*, about 3,000 tons, with a cargo of salt, from England to Singapore. The best of it was that the cargo was destined for a German firm in Singapore, and the sinking of the ship did not therefore come into question.

The *Emden* stopped. Meanwhile the English captain was enlightened by Lauterbach as to his task. He fell in with it the more readily as acceptance of the task of taking the Frenchmen to Khota Raja ensured that his ship would not be sunk.

Khota Raja, a town at the north point of the Dutch island of Sumatra, has a very well appointed hospital, and was at the time the nearest port, so we could not have done better.

The Frenchmen agreed. They had to give their word of honour not to fight against us again in this war.

The transhipment of the unwounded began first, and I went with them to the English ship so that Lauterbach should be reinforced. The slightly wounded men followed. Their transport raised no very difficult problems. The transport of those severely wounded was undertaken by our Stabsarzt, Dr. Luther in the *Emden* and Dr. Schwabe on board the English ship *Newburn*. The severely wounded men were lashed into hammocks, which made their transport easier, though the whole matter was somewhat difficult. The last of the ship's company of the *Mousquet* to be taken over was the officer. He returned grateful thanks for the excellent treatment given to his men in the *Emden*. We heard later that this officer died in Khota Raja of his severe wounds.

In the *Newburn* the wounded were stowed as

well as possible. The English captain received
exact instructions for their treatment from
Assistenzarzt Dr. Schwabe. Then we from the
Emden left the English ship. According to our
calculations the *Newburn*, at normal speed, should
reach the port of Khota Raja at eight that
evening.

The *Emden* then set a fictitious course for
Colombo, and later turned southwards, as we
intended to meet the *Buresk*.

At nine in the morning the Frenchman who
had died in the night was committed to the sea
with the same honours as had been accorded to
his two comrades.

The *Emden* was running for the agreed
rendezvous. The men were given light duties
only, and in the afternoon wash and mend
clothes.

We were to meet our companion the *Buresk*
on October 31st, and in the early morning we had
already come so near to the rendezvous that the
Buresk should come into sight at any moment.
Great care and foresight was, however, necessary,
for there was a possibility that the *Buresk* might
have been captured by a hostile warship which
was now lying in wait for us. There was therefore considerable excitement when, about
half-past four, the stern of a dark ship came in
sight.

As the huntsman stalks the buck, so did we
quietly approach this dark and questionable

object, and in spite of the darkness many sharp eyes were trying to discover what the unknown ship was like. One thing we could be certain of: the ship had only one funnel, and therefore might be the *Buresk*.

It was the *Buresk*, God be thanked. We had our companion again. Her loss would have been a hard blow, for a well-trained companion ship is a valuable object in the open sea.

She was at once signalled by Morse to follow the *Emden* on her new course. We steamed close to her, in order to exchange important news. When our Captain told her by megaphone the news of our exploit in Penang, the answer was a shout of joy.

We now steamed south-east at ten knots. In the *Emden* we had a big " clean ship," and during it all the officers assembled in the cabin for a meeting concerning the promotion of some of the men. Kapitän v. Müller wished, after the events in Penang, to promote some of the senior men who had done especially good service in the *Emden* up to this time. In particular the cutters' crews deserved some recognition, for they had borne the brunt of the capture of numerous ships and deserved to profit by it.

As the next day was a Sunday there was the usual divisions, followed by Divine Service. The order was then given: " Everybody aft ! " The promotion of about forty men was announced. Among them was the very capable Torpedomaschinistenmaat Pyttlik, who was promoted to Torpedomaschinist. He was already acquainted with his new duties. All of us in the torpedo branch were naturally delighted at this well-deserved promotion.

In a short speech the Captain emphasised that he could not promote everyone according to his deserts, but only take account of a certain number. He repeated his thanks for the good service shown by the whole ship's company.

Afterwards we were invited to a glass of champagne in the cabin, which we emptied in joyful remembrance of the success of our attack on Penang.

This first of November was an anniversary for the *Emden*. We were now three months out. The engines had made ten million revolutions, and we had put thirty thousand nautical miles behind us, with a coal consumption of 6,000 tons. With a few minor disturbances our engines had covered this long distance marvellously well. We could be grateful to the Chief Engineer, Oberingenieur Ellerbroek, for the performance of the staff and engines. Without them we could not have attained success.

In the afternoon we had complete rest. The orchestra played, and many of our men danced. The night passed without disturbance.

On November 2nd, in the early morning, we made clear for coaling, and at eight went alongside the *Buresk*. At that time we were in the neighbourhood of the Poggy Islands, west of Sumatra, and not far from the town of Padang.

Coaling began punctually at nine o'clock, and was favoured by splendid weather and a flat calm. Five hundred tons were taken in, so that the *Emden* had now 950 tons on board.

A very unpleasant accident happened among my men. We were in the full swing of coaling when a hoist broke loose high over the hatch of the hold. A few sacks of coal fell from above on to the left leg of Torpedoobermatrose Possehl, and broke his thigh. The poor fellow was at once taken on a stretcher to the sick ward, where Stabsarzt Dr. Luther put the leg in splints straight away. This was the one accident that occurred during our exploits. I am sure that none of the men were to blame for what occurred, for before the sacks were hoisted the security of the hoist was properly examined and tried.

At midday, during the meal hour, a sailing boat came alongside, from which stepped an officer in a greenish-khaki Dutch uniform. The boat, which had an auxiliary motor, made fast to the port boom. It was a captain of the Dutch colonial army, and he wished to ascertain if the *Emden* were outside the three-mile limit. We were able to assure him of this with a good conscience, and then his duty was done. He accepted gratefully an invitation to a glass of whisky and soda. His stock of news was small. The news that Portugal had also declared war on Germany awakened no great excitement in the *Emden*. The Dutchman had a sense of humour. He wished the *Emden* further good luck, and left the ship at three o'clock.

The coaling lasted till 5 p.m., when we cast off from the *Buresk* and steamed away on a westerly course. When out of sight of the island the *Emden* turned southwards. Our next objective was the Sunda Straits, where we were to cruise for a few days, and if possible effect some captures.

On November 3rd we reached the straits. We ran through and back again, but found nothing. There was not a single ship to be seen, which, properly speaking, was a result of our own activities. We had made the Indian Ocean as unsafe as possible. When cruising transversely we also came to the well-known volcano, Kvakatoa, which has blown away its former height and is broken down almost to sea level. The whole thing looked like a great hollow tooth.

Our cruise had no success because English ships dare not navigate the Indian Ocean. Something of value the *Emden* did get, however. We received, by intercepted messages, news from Dutch wireless stations which was of great interest to the *Emden*. Thus one evening we had the news that the English ship *Newburn* had run into Khota Raja with the survivors from the French destroyer *Mousquet*, and had delivered the ship's company over to the Dutch authorities. We were really glad to hear that the wounded had been brought to safety.

On November 5th we finished this cruise, and the *Emden* turned towards the appointed rendezvous with the collier *Exford*, which was to wait for us in the neighbourhood. We were steaming west, and the days passed without incident. The sea was, however, rough, and the gallant *Emden* rolled heavily in the strong swell. For seamen this was a matter of custom, and made little impression. It was unpleasant, however, for the mess steward carrying the dishes.

On November 7th we reached the appointed rendezvous, but nothing was seen of the *Exford*. We were therefore anxious about the possibility of an attack, however far the rendezvous might be from the shipping routes.

The locality had to be searched thoroughly, and we were rewarded, for on November 8th in the early morning a smoke cloud was sighted, which on nearer approach turned out to be our long-sought *Exford*.

An exchange of personnel was to be carried out. Kapitänleutnant Gropius, our Navigating Officer, was to return to the *Emden*, and Lauterbach, who, owing to his knowledge of the place, had been Navigating Officer for the attack on Penang, was to command the *Exford*. Lieutenants Fikentscher and Schall went to the *Buresk*, and Lieutenants Gyssling and Schmidt returned to the *Emden*.

The two latter were to be employed in our enterprise against the Cocos Islands, and thus take part in one warlike operation. The Signalmaat from the *Buresk* exchanged with the Signalgast from the *Exford*, as the former was to install the wireless plant in the *Exford*.

Assistenzarzt Dr. Schwabe visited a case of sickness in the *Exford*. An important matter was also the correlation of the time-keeping instruments in the three ships. The differences between the two chronometers had been the only reason why the *Exford* had not been at the rendezvous at the right time.

Accompanied by the two colliers, the *Emden* proceeded in a south-westerly direction. At four in the afternoon the *Exford* was detached, a new rendezvous having been fixed, this time in the western part of the Indian Ocean. Our Captain intended to continue the war on merchant shipping in the neighbourhood of the Island of Socotra.

The *Emden* then set a course for the so-called Direction Island, the principal island of the Cocos Group. The *Buresk* accompanied us. We went at reduced speed, as we did not wish to appear at Direction Island before daybreak.

Our plan was as follows : A landing party under command of the First Officer, Kapitänleutnant v. Mücke, was to be landed on the island, and was to destroy completely the wireless and cable stations there, and their plant. The cable station was of particular importance, being a relay station of the two cables, Australia—India and Australia —Zanzibar—Africa. If the cable were destroyed here, disquiet would be aroused in Australia as well. The enterprise was not so simple. To make a cable quite useless it is necessary to cut it, and to remove one of the cut ends to as great a distance as possible and hide it. The object is only attained if the destroyed cable cannot be found without trouble.

The destruction of a wireless station is considerably easier, as it is sufficient to destroy the wireless mast and the sending and receiving apparatus.

November 8th was principally employed in drawing up the landing party. As stated, Kapitän-leutnant v. Mücke was to have command of it. He was supported by Leutnants Gyssling and Schmidt. The party itself was composed of thirty seamen and fifteen technical ratings, with two men from the wireless staff. The landing party, including officers, was therefore fifty strong. Among the seamen were most of our " nine-year men "—that is, those who wish later to become subordinate officers and have undertaken to do nine years' service.

At seven in the evening the *Buresk* was detached. She was to wait at a distance of thirty nautical miles from the Cocos Islands, and when she received the order : " Close up ! " was to make for Direction Island.

The *Emden* had to act with all possible care, and take account of all possibilities, including that enemy warships might be lying off the Cocos Islands. Without the *Buresk* the *Emden* had more freedom of movement, which in the case of an encounter with hostile warships was necessary.

CHAPTER XII

A T six in the morning of November 9th we approached our objective, disguised with our fourth funnel, in the hope that we should be able to take the main steps unrecognised. We anchored in the entrance, and the landing party was at once piped away. The steam-pinnace and the two cutters were lowered into the water with the men in them. Kapitänleutnant v. Mücke commanded the party from the steam-pinnace. Leutnant z. S. Gyssling was in the first cutter, and Leutnant z. S. Schmidt in the second. Each cutter was armed with two machine-guns. The steam-pinnace towed the boats to land. All were flying the German flag. The party was landed shortly before seven.

The favourable weather allowed our Captain to use this time for coaling. The order was therefore sent by wireless for the *Buresk* to close up.

No answer came from the *Buresk*. The island station asked what ship was using wireless.

Naturally the *Emden* gave no answer, and our wireless staff were ordered to destroy or interfere with any messages sent out by the island station. The station did, however, succeed in sending out the message : " Foreign ship in harbour."

This was annoying, and could have been avoided if the *Emden's* guns had opened fire on the wireless station before the landing, but our Captain wished to avoid unnecessary bloodshed, and therefore directed that the wireless station alone be destroyed.

Shortly afterwards the great wireless mast of the land station was seen to topple over, as a result of blasting, which ended all further activity for the station. This was good, as a few minutes later we intercepted a wireless message from a quite unknown ship calling the land station. Measurements showed that this ship must be a good 250 sea miles away, so that there was no danger.

The *Buresk* had been called up by wireless, and we expected to meet her at about ten o'clock. At nine we sighted a smoke cloud, which we connected with the *Buresk*.

The work of the landing party lasted a very long time.

In the meantime the *Emden* was all clear for coaling.

The smoke cloud to northward suggested no doubt that the *Buresk* was approaching, for she would come from that direction. We, however, kept the arrival under close observation. Shortly afterwards followed the report that this ship had one funnel and two masts. That was like the *Buresk*. Leutnant v. Guerard went into the crow's-nest and confirmed the report.

At 9.15 a signal was sent to the landing party

that on account of exceeding the time allowed they were to hurry and bring their work to a conclusion.

A few minutes later it was reported that the ship approaching, which we had taken for the *Buresk*, had the tall masts of an English warship. Immediately afterwards the ship showed the English White Ensign.

There was now no possible doubt as to what was before us—a hard and heavy fight with the Englishman !

However hard the fight, our confidence in the fighting power of our ship and the proved leadership of our Captain was so great, that every man in the *Emden* hoped to win through again, to endure the fighting honourably, and to gain the victory.

The Captain gave the order : " Clear ship for Action ! " At the same time the siren sounded for the hasty recall of the landing party.

Minutes were precious and could not be recalled. There was no time to wait for the return of the landing party. Steam must be got up in all boilers. The *Emden* must be able to use her full speed.

At 9.30 the *Emden* weighed anchor, and steamed towards the enemy.

All this I could watch from the deck, but then duty called me to my action station in the torpedo flat, where everything was already in place. I reported this to the conning-tower. The connections for the tubes were tested once again, and everything done with dutiful thoroughness and the solemn joy of battle.

From the quivering of the ship, caused by the rapid working of the engines, we could at once tell that the *Emden* was going at full speed, and it was not long before our guns opened fire. The answer was awaited with suspense. At first nothing could be heard of enemy hits. Apparently the Englishman was shooting badly.

Towards ten o'clock there were one or two hits in the neighbourhood of the torpedo flat, and I had soundings taken in the double bottom and the compartments to find out whether water was coming into the lowest compartments of the ship. Only in this way is it possible to get a clear idea of the effect of hits below the water-line.

At 10.20 there was a diagonal hit on the armoured deck below the water line. The explosion was powerful, and the shock was so great that our Torpedomaschinist, an unusually big and strong man, measured his length on the plates. It was so comical that, in spite of the seriousness of the position and the fight for life or death, we could not restrain our laughter.

This shell made a rent in the armoured deck, through which water and the explosion gases were able to enter the torpedo flat. We of the torpedo branch therefore put on our smoke bandages—gas masks were not then known—and they did good service.

My men then tried to stop up the rent in the armoured deck, for which they used shores, covers and planks, which were stored in the torpedo flat.

It was a temporary expedient. For this work I asked for some carpenters, but could not get them as they were already occupied elsewhere. The repairs we had done ourselves were not sufficient. Water and gas were bound to leak through in time. I released some of the compressed air from the reservoir, usually used for filling the torpedo tubes, to drive out the dangerous gases, the water we could not avoid. The air was soon better. The reservoir had now to be supplied with more air, and I gave the order for this to the port auxiliary engine-room, where the torpedo air pumps are, but received no answer from there. This could only be due to the fact that the port auxiliary engine-room was out of action, and I reported this to the conning-tower.

The hits being made on our ship proved that the English had now got well into their shooting. Various shells landed on the armoured deck above the torpedo flat, and caused a great uproar with their incredibly loud explosions. We were surprised that the armoured deck still held out under such shooting. It was impossible to get news from the conning-tower, for which we in the torpedo flat were naturally very anxious. The officers there had more important work and were in continuous suspense and activity.

From time to time we were called up : " Torpedo flat," and answered : " Torpedo flat all clear ! "

At 10.25 we received the order : " Starboard tube ready ! "

This tube was at once made ready for firing. Our satisfaction was great, as we hoped to be able to join in the fight with our weapon as well. Unfortunately the opportunity never came.

My men worked splendidly. The work went forward as if at drill, though it was hindered by the water which had come into the flat. We were already up to the ankles in water. The water was set in motion by the turning and twisting of the ship till it rushed like a wave across the flat. This would have been unpleasant if the tubes had to be reloaded, as the reloading had to be done quickly, and the men might easily slip and fall in the water, which threatened unavoidable injury.

At about 10.45 we received an enormous shock, which could not have been the result of a shot as it was too dull. Our guess, that the foremast had been shot away, was later fully confirmed. We were preserved from dangerous hits. Several shells exploded above the armoured deck, but none pierced the armour after the first full hit.

Towards eleven another enemy shell found the armoured deck below the water-line. The first perceptible effect was the extinction of all lights in the torpedo flat. The emergency lighting was quickly lighted which then made it possible gradually to estimate the damage. The rent was not broad, but about 16 in. long, and we could see the water shining through it. Through the hole water and gas were again pouring into the flat. Three of my men had been wounded in the foot by shell

splinters, thank God only slightly. For lack of
material the repair of the large hole was not to be
thought of. The poisonous gas had poured in
to such an extent that we could no longer remain
in the torpedo flat. The danger of gas poisoning
had become too great, and the gas bandages were
not much use. I therefore reported to the conning-
tower : " Forced by danger from gas and water
to abandon the torpedo flat." At the same time
I gave my men the order to leave the flat.

We now tried to get above through the
armoured hatch, but could not accomplish this
as the coaming was bent. This coaming is a
band, 8 in. high, running round the hatch,
to prevent the water reaching the flat directly
the hatch should be fractured. The armoured
hatch was therefore barred to us, and there was
nothing left but to get on deck by the torpedo
transport hatch, through which torpedoes are
passed into the flat. Before this I had the
armoured hatch closed, so that the water from
the torpedo flat could not pass higher. The
people nearest, of whom I was one, therefore
rushed to the port torpedo tube, and the first
man there was hoisted up, to loosen the nuts.
The cover was then lifted off by men standing
near, whom we called. The first man was then
lifted somewhat higher, till he could be drawn
up from above. We others followed in the same
way, and I had the cover replaced, the bolts
fastened, and the whole thing secured from above.

In the waist I found a number of wounded, who
were being bandaged by Oberhoboistenmaat
Wecke, and who quickly told me how things
looked in our beloved *Emden*. Going farther
along the upper deck I then saw for myself a
frightful amount of damage, everywhere dead
and severely wounded men—everywhere groaning
and moaning and plaintive cries for help. The
most distressing part was the realisation that
there was nothing one could do, and that the
pain could not be assuaged, for everything was
a heap of wreckage. Wherever one's glance fell
one saw only holes in the side, bent pieces of metal,
burning rubbish and ashes. Our once trim *Emden*
was a ghastly sight.

In the fore battery I found Oberleutnant
Geerdes, who was wounded ; he pointed out to
me our Gunnery Officer, Gaede. Gaede was
lying at the port gun breathing his last breath,
dying fully conscious, for he still recognised me.
His uniform was red with blood. He dozed
while he was thanking me for the words of comfort I gave him, and was then carried on to the
forecastle, where he soon afterwards closed his
eyes for ever. His body was committed to the
sea, according to seamen's custom.

In the meantime the beloved Emden, *shot to
pieces and with her engines stopped, was run
aground on the south side of North Keeling Island
by her captain, Fregattenkapitän v. Müller.*

On deck a terrible picture of wreckage met my

eyes. Everything was lying tossed together; what was destructible destroyed, two funnels completely demolished, and the foremast thrown over the port side by a full hit, lying across the railing with its point in the water. By the last mentioned hit Leutnant v. Guerard, our Adjutant, and a signalman had been thrown overboard.

Everywhere lay the wounded and dead, and the groaning and cries of the former caught at one's heart, and filled one with the bitterest regret, for first-aid materials were lacking, and the best will in the world could do little to help. It was not possible to get into the first-aid room (the steering flat).

The worst was in the stern of the ship, where no one could go, because the whole deck and the side of the ship were red-hot, and fires were burning everywhere.

I was very anxious for my friend and comrade, v. Levetzow, whose action station was aft. To search for him was at first quite impossible.

Near the conning-tower I found our Captain, Kapitän v. Müller, to whom I at once reported myself and told him that all my men from the torpedo flat, with the exception of a few light wounds, were safe.

He was visibly glad to see me again safe, for he had believed that the torpedo flat had been hit far worse than it had. Naturally we were not looking beautiful, with our faces sooty and blackened, and our uniforms lemon-yellow with

the effects of shell explosions, which produce an
astonishing amount of yellow gas.

Slowly the unwounded officers assembled, and
of our total number half were missing !

What I heard from my comrades, who had
experienced the fearful fighting on deck, I give
below, so that the reader may have a clear
picture of the Emden's last fight.

At the order, " Clear ship for Action," which
was given at 9.30 a.m., Kapitän v. Müller, the
Gunnery Officer, Kapitänleutnant Gaede, the
first Torpedo Officer, Oberleutnant z. S. Witthoeft, who was also officer for manœuvres in
action, and Leutnant z. S. Zimmermann, who
was to assist the Gunnery Officer by taking
charge of certain instruments, went into the
conning-tower.

There were also there a Feuerwerksmaat and
a man to pass orders in the gunnery branch, and
the others whose action stations were there,
including the Action Helmsman. In the " fire
lee," that is on the side of the conning-tower
away from the action, were the Navigating
Officer, Kapitänleutnant Gropius, the helmsman,
and the signalman. On the quarter-deck, the
after gun control, was my friend and companion,
Oberleutnant z. S. v. Levetzow. Oberleutnant
z. S. Geerdes had command of the fore battery,
and Leutnant z. S. and Adjutant v. Guerard
was in the fore crow's nest with a signalman.
Guerard's duty was the observation of the effect

of our shooting, and the giving of information to the conning-tower about it, so that the direction, range and deflection might be passed correctly to the guns.

Orders were passed to the individual guns by means of electric transmitters. Naturally there were also reserve arrangements, such as speaking-tubes, etc.

Our chief engineer, Oberingenieur Ellerbroek, had command of the engine room and boiler. Under him was Ingenieur Andresen, who had charge of the caulking party in the midships flat, Ingenieur Haas, who was in direct charge of the boiler rooms, and Ingenieur Stoffers, who, however, on account of illness, went under cover in one of the boiler rooms.

Stabsarzt Dr. Luther was in charge of the dressing station. His action station was one of the boiler rooms. Dr. Schwabe had his station in the steering flat, which was a reserve dressing station. Oberzahlmeister Woytschekowsky was under him, and had his action station also in the steering flat.

The *Emden* left at 9.30, with her mast-head flags set, and steamed north-west.

The English cruiser, approaching the *Emden* at full speed, was at first thought to be the English light-cruiser *Newcastle*, as she had three funnels. This class of cruiser is slightly superior to the *Emden* in speed and armament, but under favourable circumstances we could have settled with such a cruiser without very great loss or damage.

At 9.35 the Englishman turned to starboard, forcing us into a running fight. The direction of the wind was favourable to us.

Five minutes later the range had narrowed from 13,000 to 10,000 yards. Kapitän v. Müller now gave the order to "Open fire." Thus the *Emden*, in spite of her inferiority in speed, opened the fight. Our opponent was the faster, and had also steam up in all boilers, whereas we had only a short time ago begun to get steam up in all boilers, and it would be a quarter of an hour before we could get steam enough in the engines for full speed.

We had hardly opened fire when the Englishman began to shoot, using for ranging purposes the fore and after guns, which confirmed us in the belief that our opponent was the *Newcastle*.

Our first two salvoes went over, and the third as well, except for one hit. We later heard that it carried away the Englishman's range-finder and all his gear. The next shots were short at first, but then correct. In order to allow our 4·1 in. guns to work more effectively, the Captain turned two points to starboard after the first salvoes At 9.53 he again turned two points to starboard.

In the beginning the Englishman shot badly. Seven or eight salvoes went over, and four or five were short. The short salvoes were a great hindrance to our observation, as the splashes continually came over the ship, obscuring our glasses, and rendering good observation very difficult.

From the columns of water thrown up by the shells we realised that they were all of the same bore, namely 5·9 in. It was therefore clear that our opponent could not be a ship of the *Newcastle* class, but a modern cruiser. What ship it was we only discovered considerably later.

The swell, now that we were out of the shelter of the island, was very noticeable.

After the *Emden's* eighth salvo there was a fire in the enemy cruiser, caused by one of our shells which had gone into a store of ammunition and set it alight. Unfortunately this explosion did not do any great or decisive damage.

Our gunlayers shot very well. If we had had bigger bored guns the fight would at least have been more favourable for us.

Fairly soon the enemy's guns got into their stride, and the first enemy hits found the *Emden* soon after ten o'clock. The first hit struck the wireless cabin, which disappeared completely. Its remains were dust and ashes. The men on duty in it were killed outright. The second exploded near the conning-tower, between the foremast and the after side of the forecastle. One of the splinters hit the helmsman Mönkediek in the left forearm, and wounded him severely. The arm was quickly bound up, and the helmsman continued his duties.

Almost at the same time a shell landed just forward of the conning-tower with very considerable effect. The guns' crews on the forecastle were disabled, along with some signalmen. Unfortunately no help could be brought to the wounded, as the first-aid party were fully occupied elsewhere, and the rest of the ship's company so tied to their posts that they could not leave them.

Now that the Englishman was shooting well, hit after hit got home on our poor ship. Almost every minute news reached the conning-tower of a disablement at a gun, or some place near one.

Soon afterwards the electric transmitters for the guns gave up work, which was a great hindrance. The Gunnery Officer had now to pass his orders through the speaking-tubes, which had, however, also been hit, so that it was very difficult to get orders through. The natural consequence was that the battery shooting, which up to now had been well together, became irregular, rendered observation very difficult, and effective shooting, that is, shooting which would effectively check the enemy, was no longer to be thought of.

The enemy now had command of the situation. With her advantage in guns and speed she could arrange for the necessary effect of her own shooting without running any danger of really damaging hits from us. From the beginning our disadvantage was our weaker armament. For our 4·1 in. guns the highest range at which effective shooting could be carried out was 7,600–8,700 yards. If our opponent maintained a greater distance effective shooting was no more to be thought of, whereas the enemy, with 5·9 in. guns, could destroy us completely.

Further casualties were reported, and then both safeguards of our electric lighting were shot away. The steering telegraph and the steering gear in the conning-tower both broke down, as the leads had probably been destroyed somewhere. The ship was now steered from the steering flat, and the engine-room telegraph was worked from the midships flat. Marine ingenieur Andresen was in command in the midships flat, and he also commanded the caulking party from there. This is really the post of the First Officer. As Kapitän-leutnant v. Mücke was ashore with the landing party at Direction Island, Andresen was representing him at this very important post.

Some minutes later the foremost funnel received a full hit, which threw it over to port. This was damaging for us as the smoke from the boilers could not be drawn off properly. This had an unfavourable effect on the speed. The fire in the furnaces had not sufficient draught. Sufficient heat could not be got up, and sufficient steam was not produced to steam at full speed. The *Emden's* speed, in any case lower than that of the enemy, was still further reduced.

Owing to the continuous hail of shells the

THE WRECKED FORECASTLE AND CHARTHOUSE OF THE "EMDEN"

losses in the guns' and magazines' crews were so severe that the guns could hardly be manned. Our guns, however, still shot with astonishing exactness and speed, but this could not last for long. Ammunition was now reaching the guns only sparely, so that lack of ammunition would be felt any minute. In fact the fire began to drop off slowly, and only a few guns were occasionally in action. The guns themselves were intact, but the munition hoists were mostly shot away, so that only after great efforts could ammunition be got up on deck.

Owing to lack of mechanical appliances, which had been rendered completely useless, it was necessary to handle everything, and therefore a large number of men were needed for the transport of munitions alone, and as these men had to carry on their work unprotected the losses were terribly severe. There were no more reserves, and it would not be long before there were no more men for the guns and ammunition-carrying.

At many guns there was now only a single man, who served his gun in fear of death. The faithfulness and heroism of these men was most evident. The heroes kept their posts to the bitter end. Several worked imperturbably in spite of severe wounds, among them a Bootsmannsmaat who had had his right arm shot away. This warrior continued to serve his gun with the arm remaining to him, as if nothing had happened to him.

At about 10.5 the steering gear again broke down, and the navigating officer and a few men rushed aft to get to the hand-steering gear. Nothing, however, answered, and when this had been reported to the conning-tower, steering was carried on by means of the ship's screws. Through this breakdown the *Emden* had made a turn hard a-starboard, so that the enemy could now rake our port side. This change was very unpleasant for us, as the enemy got in three full hits which did a great deal of damage. The first landed near the bridge, shot away our range-finding gear, and killed the people employed there. Leutnant z. S. Zimmermann thereupon left the conning-tower and went to the port gun in the forecastle, where a shell must have killed him, for he was found dead near this gun after the fight. The second hit killed the remaining men at the guns forward of the conning-tower. Some of them were already severely wounded. Several splinters entered the conning-tower through the loop-holes, and wounded the Gunnery Officer, Kapitän-leutnant Gaede, the Torpedo Officer, Ober-leutnant z. S. Witthoeft, and two more men. At this point Captain v. Müller must also have received one or two splinters, which he discovered later. The two wounded men left the conning-tower, as in consequence of the destruction of all the instruments they had no further work. They went to be bandaged, but were killed on the way to the dressing station.

The third hit, however, did the most damage, as it caught the ammunition placed ready at the fourth port gun, exploded it, and killed and burnt in the fearful flames all the men near it. Among them fell my friend Levetzow, at his post on the quarterdeck. Anything inflammable caught fire, so that after this hit the whole after part of the ship was in flames.

The Navigating Officer, Kapitänleutnant Gropius, was wounded, but could not get forward, together with a few survivors of the after guns, being completely cut off by the fire. The burning spread, so that this little group had to retreat aft. Finally there was nothing to do but jump overboard, if they did not wish to be burnt. Before their jump Gropius gave three cheers for the War Lord. The heroes joined in cheerfully and then jumped. Three of them were rescued after the end of the fight, and from them we learnt the story of these events.

Meanwhile there were more severe losses. The port guns also became silent one after another, for lack of personnel.

When Kapitän v. Müller saw that the guns had been overcome he tried, as the *Emden's* last hope, to get near enough to the enemy to be able to try the success of a torpedo. It was at this moment that we in the torpedo flat had received the order mentioned above: " Starboard tube ready ! "

The time was 10.25. Unfortunately it was

impossible to fire the torpedo, since the speed of the enemy, which at times attained twenty-seven knots, prevented us from getting within torpedo range. The distance was for the most part 7,600 yards, and to put in an effective shot we had to get to within eleven hundred yards. Our speed was low, and further reduced by the destruction of the funnel and insufficient steam. The rudder was not answering at all, and manœuvring with the screws took away a great deal of power, which still further reduced our speed.

During the manœuvre for torpedo range the enemy had again got on to our starboard side. There was nothing more for them to overcome, for our guns were now almost silent. Only now and then was a single shot fired. Suddenly the Englishman turned to port and fired a torpedo at us (the time was 10.35). The range at the time was something more than 3,200 yards. The Englishman, with her modern torpedo weapons, could also fire at greater range, though 3,200 yards is very long for a torpedo. There could be no surprise about it, and the shot failed.

The whole thing was now only a game for the enemy. The guns of the *Emden* no longer threatened, and the Englishman avoided a torpedo by steering a zigzag course (our torpedo weapons were still intact). Finally the enemy turned to starboard and steamed away at high speed.

Shortly afterwards our Gunnery Officer left the conning-tower, as control from there had become

impossible. He tried to get up a constant stream
of fire again by bringing together all the survivors
of the guns' crews and taking control himself
from near the guns. He succeeded in manning
two guns, but the effect of this last attempt was
almost nothing, for the enemy kept at a safe
distance and maintained a steady fire on the
vanquished *Emden*.

The enemy shells were hits, and again caused
great losses and damage. At about 10.45 the
foremast was shot away to port, whereby, as
already stated, Adjutant Leutnant z. S. v. Guerard
and a signalman came to their end. Another hit
wrecked the captain's bridge. In addition our
guns were now completely silenced, from which
it was certain that our Gunnery Officer must be
mortally wounded. Before, however, our Captain
completely gave up the fight, he wished to make
another attempt to get within torpedo range.
This manœuvre was rendered more difficult by
the fact that the communications between the
conning-tower and the starboard engines had
failed, and all orders had to be passed by a gunnery
transmitterman, who called the orders passed to
him down the engine-room skylight. In spite of
the hail of shells orders were passed regularly,
and the seaman concerned was not even slightly
wounded.

This last attempt to attain some positive
success against the enemy was a complete failure,
as the Englishman steered clear of every attempt

to approach her, and kept at a respectful distance from our torpedoes.

In this manœuvre also both the remaining funnels were shot away, so that our already small speed was reduced to a minimum. That meant the end for us, for what had we left to fight with ? Guns and torpedoes were both rendered useless by the failure of our speed.

This was the moment at which Kapitän v. Müller decided to run the *Emden* on to the coral reefs of North Keeling Island. This had two great advantages. Firstly, the *Emden* would not fall into enemy hands, and, secondly, a number of lives would be saved. If the ship were to sink a large part of the men, who had action stations under the armoured deck, and also all the severely wounded, would certainly be drowned without hope of rescue.

In order to put this manœuvre properly into effect the starboard engines were stopped for a time, and we then ran straight for the island. Our speed was still about nineteen knots.

The enemy had scarcely recognised our intention when he tried to sink us by an increased rate of fire, and crossed our bows in the hope of cutting off our way to the island. By this manœuvre our port side came into action again.

There was now an absolute hail of hits, but, thank God, the *Emden* remained seaworthy in spite of them. Many more of our men lost their lives at this point.

The Englishman wished to destroy us completely before we could run aground. He doubtless wanted to enjoy the triumph of seeing the *Emden* vanish into the depths, but this was denied him. When he saw that our ship was not hindered in her run for the island he had to give us room whether he wanted to or not, as otherwise he was in danger of receiving a torpedo from us or of being rammed.

Shortly before we ran aground my report reached the conning-tower that a shell had pierced the armoured deck on the starboard side above the torpedo flat, and that the flat would have to be abandoned owing to danger from gas and water.

At 11.15 the *Emden*, with her engines stopped, ran on to the south coast, in this case the lee side, of North Keeling.

In the meantime our companion the *Buresk* had come into the neighbourhood and was making vain efforts to draw off the enemy.

After running aground the engines were again put to "full speed ahead," so that the *Emden* might be firmly fixed on the coral reef. The engines were then stopped, fires were drawn and the sea-cocks opened. Our gallant *Emden*, in whom we had achieved so much success, was thus a complete wreck.

We now lay there quite unarmed, but the English ship continued her fire for another five minutes. Only at 11.20 did she cease fire.

This continued shooting at a wreck prompted our Captain to give the ship's company permission to jump overboard and try to reach the island, about 100 yards distant, by swimming. This was not easy, as there was a strong surf over the coral reef.

Shortly after this permission was given I arrived on deck, and was therefore an eyewitness of subsequent events.

I did not avail myself of the permission to jump overboard, as all possible help was wanted for the relief of the wounded. The guns had also to be made useless, and all aiming gear, secret books and measuring instruments destroyed.

The locks were taken out of the guns and thrown overboard, and the sights and measuring instruments suffered the same fate. The secret books were burnt, and also the war log-book.

As there were many severely wounded men lying about the ship, I and a few men tried to get aft from the waist, between decks. We could not, however, get farther than the engine-room hatch. The heat aft was still so great, and the metal was still glowing in such a way, that to enter must have resulted in severe burns.

Everything looked very bad there. A hit had pierced the side of the upper coal bunker in the gangway, and the whole of the coal had rolled into the gangway and almost completely blocked it. There was nothing to be done but to creep over the coal. In the laundry we found two of

our Chinese washermen, dead on the deck. They
had been surprised by a shell during the washing.
They can certainly not have been thinking of any
such end, as the *Emden* had always got well away.
These Chinese had the greatest confidence in our
luck, for when we were going into a fight they
regularly said : " Makee boom boom ! Masky ! "
which is to say : " Keep firing—never mind ! "
These two Chinese lay, like many of our gallant
men, dead on the spot where they had expired in
the execution of their duty.

From here we tried to get farther aft, but had
to give up and return to the fore part of the ship,
on account of the unbearable heat, glowing metal,
and the water which had quickly run in. We
discovered a few wounded, however, and brought
them up to the others.

Coming to the transport hatch into the torpedo
flat, I had the cover taken off to see how far the
water had come up. The flat was already full.
If we had been forced to stay there after the
second hit we could not have avoided drowning.

I then returned to the deck. In the meantime
all the severely wounded men had been brought
on to the forecastle. Bandages were applied as
far as they would go. As they did not last out
we took the bed linen and table-cloths, which
were of good linen and did very good service.

A few men had availed themselves of the
permission to swim to the island. The attempt
looked easier than it was. The difficulty was the

very heavy surf. It fell on the reef with colossal force, and many men had their heads dashed on the coral and lost their lives. In spite of their physical strength this fate was shared by Assistenzarzt Dr. Schwabe, and by my torpedo-maschinist Pyttlik. Both were found on the shore of the island a day later with their skulls broken, the maschinist dead and the surgeon dying.

Of our opponent we had only so far been able to make out that she was an Australian cruiser of the Melbourne class, and was making no preparations to send the *Emden* life-boats. Rather she was making off after the *Buresk*. We therefore sought for means to get into communication with the island, in the interest of our wounded who had to have water. The water tanks above the armoured deck were shot away, and the drinking-water compartments were under the torpedo flat, which was full of sea-water. We could not get to these compartments, and the pumps were not going, partly because they had been damaged, and partly because the fires had been drawn. The small amount of drinking water remaining in the pipes was used down to the last drop, so as at least to moisten the fever-parched tongues of the severely wounded men.

We hoped to find a sufficient quantity of coco-nuts on the island, and to be able to quench the men's thirst with their milk. Everyone suffered greatly from the severe heat on deck,

The sailcloth and other material used for protection from the sun was stowed in compartments which were under water and could not be reached.

We had no boats in which to reach the island. Some of our boats had been taken by the landing party, and the pinnace, which remained on board the *Emden*, had been burnt. A few of our men, who had reached the island by swimming in spite of the surf, could now help to establish some link with the *Emden*. We tried to float a thin line over to the beach by means of empty ammunition boxes and matting. This line was to be caught by the men on the shore. It was intended to bend on a stronger hawser to this line and thus pull it to the beach. The current, however, prevented our floats reaching the shore. The attempt did succeed once, but the men on the shore were not quick enough and the line parted on the sharp edges of the coral. All our other attempts with floats failed, and we had as little luck with the life-saving rifle, with which a thin line can be shot to a fair distance. Finally it was decided that two of the *Emden's* best swimmers should try to get the line to the island. They tied it round their bodies and did their best to swim through the surf, but did not succeed, and had to return to the ship with their task unaccomplished.

Careful observation showed that there was only one place where it was possible to cross the reef by swimming, but this place lay much too far from the ship.

The luck had left us, and our miseries on board increased.

The severely wounded men were tended with the greatest care, and in a few hopeless cases morphia had to be given to lessen the terrible pain. As soon as we had treated one patient and left him for the next, he was at once assailed by gulls. This was a kind of gull known as "Döskoppe," and they hovered over the helpless cases and attacked their eyes. These unpleasant birds were killed off as far as possible with cudgels and short-range pistols.

In the afternoon at about four o'clock the enemy cruiser returned from the chase of our companion. We later heard that the Englishman had captured the *Buresk*, but only in a sinking condition. Kapitänleutnant Klöpper, on the approach of the enemy, opened the sea-cocks and threw the valves themselves overboard.

I was standing on the shattered bridge of our poor *Emden* to watch what move the returning enemy would make. She was towing two of the *Buresk*'s boats, and stopped exactly astern of us, at about 4,000 yards distance. The expectation that the enemy would now send us boats was not at first fulfilled. Instead, an international signal went up which, for lack of a signal-book, we could not read. On the Captain's order a signalman returned the Morse flag signal: " No signal-book ! " (in English).

What they understood by it I do not know.

Suddenly, to our great astonishment, the English-man began to fire on us. I saw the smoke puff out fore and aft, reported it at once to the Captain, and hurried down from the bridge, as I had no desire to be caught by a shell splinter.

I had scarcely got below when the first shell arrived. A stoker standing near me sank down without a sound. A splinter had caught him in the back of the head and killed him instantly.

Kapitän v. Müller at once announced : " Who-ever can swim may jump overboard if he wishes ! "

Many of the men availed themselves of this permission, and I also jumped overboard to port, seized a floating plank and tried to get through the surf to land. Thank God there were no sharks about, for they usually abound in these waters. I think they must have been frightened away by the numerous shells exploding in the water during the fight.

The enemy shells exploded around us, and our *Emden*, already a wreck, received several more hits, which caused new fires.

Several of the ship's company who could not swim well had jumped overboard, and the better swimmers therefore tried to supply these men with planks and balks to swim with. There were several men clinging to my plank, which consider-ably affected its buoyancy. I therefore left it and swam back to the *Emden* after an attempt to swim through the surf had failed.

I was a good half-hour in the water, and in the

meantime the enemy had ceased fire. In the *Emden* the ensign was hauled down and the white flag run up.

Later the English newspapers stated, in their articles about the final fight, that Kapitän v. Müller surrendered. This was incorrect. One can only surrender with weapons! As, however, our ship was a wreck, and all weapons on board had been destroyed, there could be no talk of surrender. The flag was hauled down because a wreck has no longer any right to fly it, and further bloodshed was useless and could not be justified. On running on to the reef the flag had been forgotten, as, God knows, other work was more pressing, and it did not occur to any of us that a flag at the maintop of a wreck would be taken as a reason for resuming the bombardment.

This attack on a wreck claimed several more victims. It was a wonder that a shell did not strike the forecastle, where the wounded were lying, and where a large number of officers and men were attending as far as possible to their wounds.

The affair was described by our comrades of the *Buresk*, which to the Englishman's wrath had been sunk by our men. Our comrades, who were between the decks of the cruiser, said that their hearts stopped when they saw that fire was being opened on the wreck that had once been the *Emden*.

After the cease-fire had sounded the Australian

cruiser sent one of the *Buresk's* boats over, with Leutnant z. S. Fikentscher and some men. The cruiser herself went off towards Direction Island, no doubt with the intention of capturing the landing party under Kapitänleutnant v. Mücke.

From Fikentscher we learned the name of our opponent. She was the Australian cruiser *Sydney*. As we thought, she was going to Direction Island, and would fetch us from the *Emden* next day.

We were quite clear in our minds that in the attempt to land a party against our comrades on Direction Island the Englishmen would get some hard knocks. We knew too well the spirit of the leader, v. Mücke, and of his men. It did not seem certain to us that the Englishman would fetch us next day. We intended to redouble our efforts to establish communications with the island, and we had now one of the *Buresk's* boats to help us.

Darkness fell too soon for our attempt, and work had to be discontinued. Everyone needed rest and a chance to recuperate.

That night each man made himself as comfortable as he could on the wreck. The clear tropical sky was wonderfully beautiful, with the particular sign of the southern hemisphere, the Southern Cross, over us as we slept.

The night did not, however, pass without disturbance. Fires kept breaking out, and had at once to be extinguished. This work was led by Leutnant z. S. Fikentscher. Most of us were quite exhausted. We had had nothing to eat the whole day, and the frightful heat of the day had taken more out of us than would otherwise have been the case.

At dawn we were on our feet again. Somewhat refreshed by our short night's rest, but not in the best of humours, most of the ship's company were wondering what was to happen next. The work of establishing communications with the island left little time for grumbling.

As we were actually in distress on the wreck the international signal was hoisted : " Am in distress ! Need help ! " This was a measure of prudence. If the *Sydney* did not fetch us it was hoped that a passing ship would take pity on us.

During the morning I went on to the shattered quarterdeck. I did not wish to miss an opportunity of looking for my friend Levetzow. Near the mainmast I discovered his remains. There were only bones ; the rest was burnt. From the shape of the head and an Oberleutnant's star I was certain that it was really Levetzow. He must have been killed by the explosion of the ammunition for the after battery. His remains were committed to the sea according to nautical custom.

I had missed my friend Levetzow at the end of the fight, but it had been impossible to look for him then on account of the frightful heat in the after part of the ship. For me his loss was a very sad one. He was not only my comrade-in-arms, but in every sense a true friend, from whom I had always had good advice and help.

In the night several of the severely wounded men had died, and among them one whose whole skin was burnt. The unfortunate man suffered frightful pain. It was over now.

The attempts to link up with the land failed, but the work was not abandoned. We still had the boat, but this precious reserve was not to be used except as a last resort. We would wait and see if the Englishman returned. If not, we would use the boat.

The Englishman appeared at one o'clock midday (Nov. 10th). From the fact that her boats were swung out we could tell that she intended to take us off.

We were more assured about the future now, although the thought of captivity was depressing.

Two cutters came across under the command of an English officer, who told our Captain that the captain of the *Sydney* was willing to take our ship's company on board his ship, and also the men on the island, if Kapitän v. Müller would guarantee the suppression of hostile behaviour by the Germans while on board the *Sydney*. The Captain gave the necessary promise.

With this introduction, the transhipment of the *Emden's* ship's company began, the severely wounded men going first.

Owing to the very heavy sea towards the land there was a danger that the life-boats would be crushed against the *Emden*. Some of the seas were washing over the stern and occasionally breaking over the side on to the deck. The transhipment of the wounded was greatly hindered by this.

The boats made fast on the port side aft—that is, a stout line was passed, for to make fast properly was impossible. The crews of the English cutters showed great ability by keeping the boats in such a position that they were not dashed against the ship's side, so that the wounded could be got into the boats without giving the poor fellows too much pain. The severely wounded men were lashed into carrying hammocks and lowered carefully.

The lightly wounded men were more easily transferred, and then the uninjured men followed. Last of all, Kapitän v. Müller left his ship. With a few men he had been trying to start a fire in the neighbourhood of the magazines.

We hoped by this means to set fire to the magazines, and blow the *Emden* to pieces and sink her.

Unfortunately this attempt was unsuccessful.

The English captain had sent over his gig for Kapitän von Müller as a mark of respect. Von Müller had to accept this whether he wished to or not, although he had previously requested the omission of special honours.

Out of the ship's company who were on board during the fight we had :—

1. Killed, drowned, and died of wounds:
   7 officers, 1 marine-oberzahlmeister,
   4 subordinate officers, 25 petty officers,
   92 men, 1 civilian cook, 1 barber,
   3 Chinese washermen ;

2. Seriously wounded : 1 subordinate officer,
   3 petty officers, 17 men ;

3. Lightly wounded : 2 officers, 2 subordinate
   officers, 9 petty officers, 31 men.

There remained unhurt 6 officers, 5 subordinate officers, 39 petty officers, and 67 men.

The exploits of our unforgettable *Emden* were thus at an end. May these exploits be an example for later generations, and the spirit of the *Emden* awake again in our people the sense of loyal co-operation in joy and in trouble. If this should come to pass, our sadly oppressed Fatherland will again experience better times than those in which these lines are written ! God send it may be so !

CHAPTER XIII

BEFORE I describe how we became prisoners, a few extracts from the newspapers are inserted here, which show what a name the *Emden* and her immortal Captain, Kapitän v. Müller, made for themselves.

The reports are taken from the "Deutsche Geschichtskalender" and the collection of reports entitled "Der Völkerkrieg." Both works have collected all the material which is necessary for war books, in an exemplary manner.

"November 1st, 1914. The German light-cruiser *Emden* has, according to *The Times*, up to date sunk 15 English ships, and captured and set free again five. The English victims of the *Emden* make a total of 93,000 tons.

"On the same date H.M. the Kaiser sent to the Mayor of the town of Emden the following telegram : ' I congratulate the town of Emden on its foster-child in the Indian Ocean, whose fine cruiser work fills all German hearts with pride and joy.—WILHELM I.R.'

"On November 4th it is reported : ' The Iron Cross, first and second class, is awarded to the Captain of the *Emden*, and the Iron Cross, second class, to all officers and subordinate officers, and to fifty petty officers and men of the ship's company.'

" November 9th. ' The light-cruiser *Emden* was attacked near the Cocos Islands in the Indian Ocean by the Australian cruiser *Sydney*, while a landing party was out of the ship for the destruction of the English cable and wireless stations. Fires were started by the shells, and after a hard fight she was run aground by her own ship's company, where she burnt out. [This is not quite true. She only partially burnt out.—THE AUTHOR.] The party landed for the destruction of the cable station, 3 officers and 46 men [47 men. —THE AUTHOR], with four machine-guns, escaped in the little schooner *Ayesha*.'

" The Captain of the *Emden*, Fregattenkapitän v. Müller, sent the following report to the German Admiralty : ' The cruiser *Sydney* approached the Cocos Islands at full speed exactly as the landing party from the *Emden* succeeded in destroying the cable. The fight between the two cruisers began at once. Our shooting was at first good, but after a short time the fire from the heavy English guns gained the advantage, and caused heavy losses among our guns' crews. The ammunition came to an end and the guns had to cease fire. In spite of the fact that the steering gear was damaged by enemy fire, an attempt was made to get within torpedo range of the cruiser *Sydney*. This attempt failed, as the funnel was destroyed and the speed of the *Emden* greatly reduced in consequence. The ship was therefore run at full speed on to the reef on the north (lee) side of the Cocos Islands. [It was the south side of North Keeling Island.—THE AUTHOR.] In the meantime the landing party had succeeded in escaping in a schooner belonging to the island. The English cruiser gave chase, but returned in the afternoon and fired on the wreck of the *Emden*. To avoid unnecessary bloodshed I therefore surrendered with the rest of the ship's company. The *Emden's* losses were : 6 officers, 1 marine-oberzahlmeister, 4 subordinate officers, 26 petty officers, and 93 men killed. 1 petty officer and 7 men severely wounded.' [One officer and some men died of wounds on board the *Sydney*. The figure here does not agree, therefore with the actual losses. The civil cook and the barber are included, but not the Chinese washermen.—THE AUTHOR.]

" Telegram from the German Kaiser to the municipal representatives of the town of Emden : ' Hearty thanks for your message of sympathy on the distressing and heroic end of my cruiser, the *Emden*. The gallant ship gained further laurels for the German Ensign in her last fight. A new and stronger *Emden* will be built, on whose bows the Iron Cross will be affixed, in memory of the fame of the old *Emden*.— WILHELM I.R.'

" The announcement that the *Emden's* famous run was ended caused great grief throughout

Germany, mingled with pride at the performance
of the ship and her gallant ship's company."

The *Norddeutsche Allgem. Zeitung* writes thus:
" For three full months, under the most difficult
conditions, the *Emden*, with tenacious courage
and exemplary seamanship, has harried the
enemy and caused them heavy losses. Finally
she had to succumb to the hunt for her organised
by British, Russian, French, and Japanese warships. The name *Emden* will, however, live in
the memory of the German people to all posterity.
All honour to her officers and the valiant men
who continued till death to do faithful service
for the Kaiser and the Empire ! "

The Austrian press also published an honourable
recognition of the heroism, adventurous spirit,
and valiance of the *Emden*. Thus, for instance,
the Vienna *Fremdenblatt* : " The *Emden* has
showed the German people a magnificent example
of German valour and initiative, and has covered
the young German fleet with imperishable glory.
Austria-Hungary sends to the heroic men, who
did their utmost and best, her greetings, and is
proud to call the people an ally which has produced
such heroes. We are filled with admiration for
the audacity of the Captain, Kapitän von Müller,
and congratulate him on his initiative, which is
combined with humanity."

The Norwegian press took the same view. The
Christiania *Aftenposten* expresses its judgment
in the sentence : " The performance of the *Emden*

is without parallel in the history of the war.
No one would have believed that a single cruiser
could do so much damage in a modern war and
faced with overwhelming enemies as the *Emden*
has done. Few names have, during the war,
been so often in the mouth of the people as that
of the *Emden* and her gallant Captain.

" How the *Emden* has succeeded in procuring
the necessary supplies over so long a time is a
question at which many guesses have been made,
and which will perhaps now be solved. Whatever
the answer, it speaks of great cleverness, foresight, and administrative talent in the Captain."

In England the news of the *Emden's* end
naturally awakened the greatest joy. At Lloyd's
the premiums immediately fell by half. The
English press, however, could not avoid recognition of the fine performance of the *Emden's* ship's
company. Thus the London *Daily Chronicle*
writes : " The Captain proved himself to be not
only a brave and capable officer, but to possess
chivalry in his treatment of the crews and passengers of the captured ships. We can all take off
our hats to the Captain." [This, however, they
later did not do.—THE AUTHOR.]

The *Daily News* writes : " The English nation
has now only one regret, and that is that a great
part of the *Emden's* ship's company lost their
lives. The Captain of the *Emden* is a gallant
man, full of resource and chivalry. He treated
his prisoners very well, and played his part to

admiration. The *Emden*, like the *Alabama*, will always live in naval history."

The Times writes : " If all the Germans had fought as well as the Captain of the *Emden*, the German people would not to-day be reviled by the world." [One sees at once the spiritual parent of this paper. The chase before all !—THE AUTHOR.]

The Italian press in general gave expression to their sympathy with the German sailors and their pity for the fate of the ship. Even the *Corriere della Sera*, which, God knows, was not pro-German, wrote on November 12th, 1914 : " The only ship which despair made strong, and which embraced her inevitable fate, has won laurels for the German Navy which neither time nor fate can wither. And if the day ever comes when war shall be banished for ever, even then the *Emden's* fame will not diminish, for always, and especially with the higher development of mankind, the man who lays down his life for his duty will be the highest pattern of human virtue. This ship's company could, in Chinese waters subject to the German flag, have fought equally with other ships until surrender, without damage to their honour. That was, however, not the wish of their Captain, Karl von Müller, a name that will live. He went out with his faithful men upon a hunt, the idea of which was his alone, by which he could do the greatest possible damage to the enemy. He did not seek to avoid his fate,

but sought on the other hand to further it with
great power and audacity. Thus the *Emden* has
become the wonderful adventurer of the Indian
Ocean. Forty warships were searching for her,
and one eventually succeeded in sinking her, but
the ship herself crowned her fame when, mortally
wounded, she sank beneath the sea. The fame
of the *Emden* lives in the depths of the sea, and
in the thoughts of mankind ! "

On January 2nd, 1915, the Wolff Telegraph
Bureau announced that Captain Glossop of the
Sydney had made a report on the victory over the
Emden to the British Admiralty, who had published it. This report ran : " When on patrol
duty we received a wireless message from the
Cocos Islands, whereupon we at once laid a course
for the islands, steaming at full speed. We soon
reached a speed of twenty knots, sighted land at
9.15, and almost immediately afterwards saw the
smoke of the *Emden*, which was approaching at
great speed. She opened fire at 9.50. I kept at
the greatest possible distance in order to take
advantage of the longer range of my guns. At
the beginning of the fight the fire of the *Emden*
was very rapid and exact, but soon fell off. All
the losses in the *Sydney* occurred at the beginning
of the fight. The foremost funnel of the *Emden*
was first shot away, and then the foremast. A
large fire broke out on board, and after the second,
and finally the third, funnels had fallen, the ship
made for the beach. We fired another two

salvoes at the *Emden*, and then gave chase to
a merchant-ship which had approached during
the fight. She was the captured British collier
Buresk, manned by Germans and a few Chinese.
The Germans bored a hole in the ship, which soon
afterwards sank. The *Sydney* then returned to
the *Emden* and rescued the men who were in the
water. [Three men in all.—THE AUTHOR.] The
cruiser's flag was still flying at the mast-head.
We asked : ' Will you surrender ? ' and received
no answer, so that against our will we were forced
to open fire again at 4.30. Five minutes later,
however, we ceased fire, and commenced to rescue
the men in the water." [Not true ! If the
report actually said so its accuracy was its weakest
point.—THE AUTHOR.]

" The following day an officer had a conversation
with the Captain of the *Emden*. It was decided
to bring over to us the wounded and prisoners,
which was difficult on account of heavy surf.
The state of the *Emden* was indescribable. Eleven
officers and 200 men were taken prisoners. Among
the prisoners were 54 wounded." [As I have
already remarked, I throw doubt on the accuracy
of the report. I cannot imagine that an English
captain would make a report to his supreme
command which was full of inaccuracies. The
number of prisoners and wounded at the end is
not correct.—THE AUTHOR.]

The report of the English captain proceeds as
follows :. " The officer of the *Sydney* who talked

with Kapitän v. Müller on the day after the fight made the following report : ' At eleven in the morning we were at the place where the *Emden* was lying. [The time is not correct. It was one o'clock.—THE AUTHOR.] I was sent over with one of our boats. It was not at all easy to get on board, but with help from the Germans, who were standing in a group on the after deck, I finally got on board, and went up to Kapitän v. Müller and greeted him. I greeted him from the captain and said that if he would give his word to regard himself as a prisoner of war we would take him and his whole ship's company on board the *Sydney*, and convey them straight to Colombo. He considered this, and finally fell in with it. Then came, however, the terrible task of taking the wounded across in our boats. There were, in all, 150 men, but luckily we had very practical gear with us, and finally succeeded in getting three of the most severely wounded men into each of our boats. The Germans were all suffering from terrible thirst, so we hoisted the water breakers from our boats into the *Emden*. They rushed for them at once, but gave the wounded a drink first. As soon as I had an opportunity I went up to the German Captain and said : " The *Emden* fought splendidly." He started at the words and said shortly : " No ! " Immediately afterwards, however, he came up to me and said : " It is very friendly of you to say that, but almost at the beginning you had the luck to shoot away

my order transmitters." Later I went round the
ship, but have no great desire to describe what
I saw. With the exception of the forward gun-
wale, which was almost undisturbed, the whole
ship was like a slaughter-house. The German
doctor begged that the *Sydney* might be signalled
to send over some morphia. I did not go below
again. Among the officers, the Torpedo Officer,
W——, was a very distinguished man. Lieutenant S—— was also attractive, and he was half
an Englishman. It made a great impression when
I told them that our captain would take care that
there was no cheering when we reached Colombo,
and no celebrations. Naturally we did not wish
for that when we had on board dead and dying
enemies. Kapitän v. Müller is a splendid man.' "

" More exact news was received of the gallant
landing party which the *Emden* had left on the
Cocos Islands. According to this news the *Emden*
appeared at six in the morning in the entrance to
the lagoon, and at once lowered a barge and two
boats, which soon afterwards landed three officers
and forty men. Besides their rifles these men
had four machine-guns with them. The little
troop hurried to the telegraph station, where
they removed the telegraphists, destroyed the
instruments, and posted sentries in the building.
All knives and guns were of course taken from
the station staff. The telegraphists worked up
to the moment the German seamen broke in.
They succeeded in sending another cry for help

before the wireless apparatus was destroyed.
While the cable station was also put out of action
a party of the Germans got hold of the cable, to
cut it, and at the same time the station magazine
was blown up. The attempt to cut the cable
was not successful. At nine o'clock the siren
sounded from the *Emden* to recall the landing
party, who at once went back to the boats. They
did not leave, however, as the *Emden* was already
under way, and looking eastwards they could see
a strange warship approaching. The *Emden*
opened fire on her at 3,800 yards, at the same
time manœuvring to the northward. The more
closely the two cruisers became engaged, the
farther they went from the island, and they
finally vanished from the gaze of the landing
party, who could only see that the stern of the
Emden was in flames. The Germans thereupon
landed again, spread out along the coast of the
lagoon, and put themselves in a position for
defence against a possible landing by the English.
The cruisers lost themselves in the distance.
The Germans thereupon possessed themselves of
the schooner *Ayesha*, belonging to a Mr. Ross,
provisioned her, and sailed away." This report
was given by an inhabitant of Direction Island.

After this digression, which was necessary,
according to my opinion, in order to complete a
picture of the doings of the *Emden*, and her
influence at home and abroad, I return to our
transhipment to the *Sydney*. Naturally a mass

of newspaper articles could be brought forward,
but the small selection given will suffice for its
object.

We reached the *Sydney* after a short journey
in the boats. We were received at the boom by
Klöpper and Schall, and shown to our positions
between decks.

The severely wounded men were at once taken
in charge by the surgeons, and operated on. One
can only say that a great deal was done in this
respect, and that the first-aid staff took every
conceivable trouble to help the wounded and as
far as possible ease their pain.

We washed in the officers' bathroom, put on
fresh underclothes and tropical uniforms, which
had been placed at our disposal by the English
officers, and then received a hearty supper. How
good it tasted can be imagined when I say that
we had been hungry for 35 hours. Still better was
the well-cooled beer. We had brought with us a
thirst that was more than healthy.

The feeling that we were prisoners of war was
repugnant, but the English officers took every
trouble to mitigate our position and make us for
a time forget it. They brought us books, cigars
and cigarettes. Our sleeping quarters were in
the large ante-room of the wardroom, where we
made ourselves as comfortable as possible for the
night on the settees and in hammocks. Kapitän
v. Müller was given accommodation in the English
captain's cabin. Our men slept on the forecastle,

and the wounded in the waist, on hammocks laid on the deck. In the warm tropical nights this was the best place, as there was always fresh air. The main and side awnings were also brought out during the day.

On board the *Sydney* we heard some interesting news about the approach of the cruiser to the island. Up to then we had had no idea how the Australian cruiser came to be in the neighbourhood of the Cocos Islands. We now heard that on the morning of November 9th the English ships *Sydney* and *Melbourne* and the Japanese armoured-cruiser *Ibuki* were only fifty nautical miles north-east of the islands. These three ships were on their way from Australia to Colombo, as protection for a convoy of troop-ships, and were to proceed from there to Egypt. For the *Sydney*, with her speed, it was therefore a trifle to reach Direction Island in two hours, when she received the cry for help of the island station. Our assumption that the ship was at least 250 nautical miles away was mistaken. We sent out with full strength, but the *Sydney* with reduced power, and our wireless men had thus been deceived about the distance.

The captain of the *Melbourne* had command of the troop-transport, and on receipt of the message from the island ordered the *Sydney* to seek out the enemy and force her into a fight. For safety the two captains agreed that upon cessation of wireless communication, which was to be kept up constantly, the *Melbourne* would at once come to the *Sydney's* help.

We heard that the Japanese had wished to engage us, and pluck a few cheap laurels. She had even set her mast-head flags.

If, therefore, we had had the luck to sink the *Sydney*, we would certainly have been dealt with by her sister ship.

In proportion to the strength of the *Sydney* her losses were very small, 4 dead and 17 wounded. The ship had been hit by us about sixteen times. The events were :

Out of the second salvo of the *Emden* one shell hit but did not explode. It carried away the range-finding apparatus for the fore-fire control, and wounded all the persons employed there, including one officer. This was the reason why the *Sydney* shot so badly at the beginning of the fight. One shell exploded near the second starboard gun, and put the whole gun's crew out of action. Another hit the upper shield of the first starboard gun, but did not do much damage. By one shell some cordite was set alight in the waist. One shell exploded in the ship's boys' mess. Three hit the side armour. Here one could plainly see how laughably small was the effect of our shells at the long range. I examined one place closely. It looked as if someone had taken a heavy sledge-hammer and hit it. Further hits were made on the forecastle, in one of the starboard boats, and in the first officer's cabin.

18

One shell cut the steam pipes of the ice-machine, which stood on the battery deck. Another pierced the ventilation shaft on the boat deck, and another hit the forward side of the mainmast, but only splintered the mast slightly. The only shell which might have been effective entered an ammunition hoist, and threw burning cordite into a magazine. A seaman, however, with great presence of mind, threw the stuff aside and extinguished it. By this decisive action he burnt both his arms, but saved his ship, for if the ammunition there had exploded that hour would have been the *Sydney's* last.

On closer examination of the *Sydney* we got some idea of the strength of our opponent. All parts were well armoured and of strong construction. She had modern 5·9 in. long calibre guns, beside which our guns looked like toys.

The second piece of interesting news we heard in the *Sydney* concerned the fate of our landing party. After firing on the *Emden* for the second time the *Sydney* had gone straight to Direction Island. Captain Glossop intended to summon our landing party to surrender, and in case of a refusal to overcome them by force. A landing party was told off under the English first officer, and took with them one of our seamen from the *Buresk* as interpreter, after Leutnant z. S. Schall had refused his co-operation. Confident in their hope of a second victory the English party was towed to shore. They were astonished at being

able to reach the shore unhindered. The landing
was also completed without hindrance, and the
party was greeted joyfully by the English inhabitants. The first question naturally concerned
the German landing party. The answer was :
" The Germans have left in our schooner the
Ayesha ! "

The rage of the first officer may be imagined.
Waiting could do no good. The Germans had
finally got away.

The Englishmen took with them the station
doctor and returned to the *Sydney*. The news
of the disappearance of the Germans was at once
reported to the captain, and the English ship
cruised for a time in the neighbourhood, but could
see no trace of the fugitives.

On November 10th the *Sydney* returned from
her useless expedition to the wreck of the *Emden*,
and took us off for Colombo.

We were naturally delighted that v. Mücke
and his men had got away so nicely. Even the
English officers agreed that v. Mücke had handled
the matter very well.

In the evening of November 10th Leutnant
z. S. Schall was sent ashore on North Keeling
Island to collect all the men there before the next
morning, so that they could be brought off to the
Sydney.

Although we could not forget the events of the
last two days, the fatigue following our severe
strain made us sleep well throughout the night.

Our mood on November 11th in the morning was therefore somewhat better. In the early morning Schall returned to the *Sydney* with the men who, in spite of surf, etc., had succeeded in reaching North Keeling Island. The men looked almost mad. They were terribly hungry and thirsty, although the Englishmen had had the foresight to take fresh water with them and had given them plenty to drink. On board our islanders were at once fed, and the Englishmen gave all possible attention to the wounds they had suffered.

From Schall we heard that Assistenzarzt Dr. Schwabe, who had swum across to the island, had that night died of his wounds. He was buried on the island with the other dead who had been washed up on the shore.

These men told us that the food had been very scarce on the island. There were only coco-nuts and a few gulls' eggs, and these had been loyally shared out to the wounded by the uninjured.

After they were all on board, the *Sydney* proceeded again to Direction Island and set down the station doctor, who had reinforced the *Sydney* for a day and had done very good work among the many wounded men. She then proceeded towards Colombo.

Glad as we were of the rest after our strenuous and anxious days, we were still much concerned about our men who were seriously wounded. On November 12th two of them died, operations being useless. These were a technical petty officer, and a seaman, half of whose head had been torn away by a splinter. Marine-Ingenieur Stoffers, who, before the fight, was in sight of recovery from a long illness, had also received a number of splinters in his chest and head. All attempts to save him failed. He could not take food, and his breathing became steadily worse. He died fully conscious in the early morning of November 13th, having been served faithfully up to his death by his servant Dehorn.

Next day these three were committed to the sea. The ceremonial was very complete, and entirely corresponded with our own customs.

On the previous day an English seaman, who had died on board, had been buried in exactly the same way.

The *Sydney* was too small for our large number of wounded, and the sick-berth staff were over-worked. The captain therefore called up the auxiliary-cruiser, *Empress of Russia*, by wireless, and appointed this ship, on account of the large amount of room in her, as hospital ship. She arrived on November 14th, took over a number of our lightly wounded men, as well as all the severely wounded, and then fell into line astern.

This ship was a veritable boon to the wounded, on account of the better accommodation and attendance. They made great progress, the danger of death disappeared, and the next days passed quietly.

The arrival in Colombo occurred at about ten in the morning on November 15th. The harbour gave an impression of strength, on account of the number of warships, among which were some Japanese and the Russian cruiser *Askold*, together with a large number of troop-ships for Europe.

Towards midday those of us who had remained in the *Sydney* were taken to the hospital ship. We had scarcely assembled on deck when the first officer of the *Empress of Russia* came up to us and read an order from the War Office by which the King of England returned to us officers and subordinate officers our swords. This was in so far meaningless, as we had no swords with us, but doubtless the order was intended as an honour for the *Emden*, and as such it greatly pleased us.

According to reports received, we were to proceed to England in the *Empress of Russia*. We were glad of this news, as the ship was quite modern and well adapted for such a long journey. Most of us had a cabin to ourselves. I had one with Schall, who was of my year, and it was the more welcome to me because I had shared with Schall the whole time in the *Emden*.

The men also were well accommodated. The only disadvantage was that they were guarded by French marines. We officers, probably with intention, were guarded by English sentries.

The Frenchmen behaved very strictly to our

WRECKED COMPASS FORECASTLE BRIDGE OF THE "EMDEN"

men, and this may have been the reason why the English seamen took every opportunity of doing our men a good turn and bringing them cigarettes, chocolate, and other food. It was particularly noticeable that on the side of the French there was hate, and on that of the English a certain fellow-feeling, although we were enemies.

At about midday the wounded were landed in lighters and taken to the two hospitals. This transportation was carried out in some respects in a very unpractical manner. The lighters had not the least protection against the sun, so the poor wounded had to endure the terrible heat. We could alter nothing, and the English wounded had to undergo the same treatment, but the fact was a proof of bad organisation.

In the afternoon our stay in the *Empress of Russia* was unexpectedly brought to a sudden end, and we were transferred to the Australian and New Zealand transports. The *Empress* was not going to England, but was to remain for the time in Colombo.

Our Captain, v. Müller, Leutnant z. S. Fikentscher, Stabsarzt Dr. Luther, and I were taken to the ship *Orvieto*, of the Orient Line, together with two subordinate officers and about thirty men. Each of the other transports took two or three officers, some subordinate officers, and a corresponding number of men.

Oberleutnant z. S. Geerdes was the only wounded officer who was to remain in Colombo.

This was good, in so far as it supplied a certain supervision from the German side for the wounded we left. As it happened, Geerdes was lucky, as he was able to go home much sooner than we who were interned in Malta.

Our accommodation was very good. Each officer had a cabin on the upper deck. These cabins were next to each other, and were separated from the rest of the ship by two gratings. On either side there were sentries with side-arms.

Twice a day we were allowed to walk on part of the large promenade deck on the starboard side, accompanied by an English officer. We ate in what was formerly the nursery, again supervised by an English officer. These gentlemen were very pleasant, and only one made a somewhat laughable figure. He said not a word at table, and this offspring of Mars sat all the time with his hand on his revolver. He wished to appear martial, but could only win from us a smile of pity.

On November 17th the transport left Colombo for Aden. The English cruiser *Hampshire* had the command, but the central command proper was in the *Orvieto*, with the appropriate staff. This consisted of an Australian General with his staff, and an English naval captain, who was in command of the transport, with some Marine officers, who were given to the captain as his staff.

The voyage to Aden was pleasant on the whole,

though we were often reminded that we were prisoners of war. Whenever, for instance, we wished to go to a certain place, it was not so easy to do so. We had to call a sentry, who first planted his side-arms under one's nose. When we had communicated our humanly comprehensible wish to him, the strong locks were unlocked, and we were let through. We could not, however, go alone, but were faithfully accompanied thither, and our companion remained before the door so long as we were inside. Otherwise the " danger " to the ship would have been too great, or perhaps these " ingenious Germans " would have made an attempt at escape on the high seas.

This procedure was still worse in the case of the men, for the door could not be shut, and the sentry stationed himself opposite the door, and supervised the whole proceeding.

No communication was possible between officers and men. As far as I can remember Kapitän v. Müller, during the long voyage, was only once allowed to see his men. The reasons for this remain unknown to me, but I believe I may assume that the military authorities had a very wholesome respect for us. This impression was often confirmed during my time as prisoner of war.

During the whole voyage we had the most splendid weather. For lack of work one idled the whole day. I played cards or chess with Fikentscher. The rest of the time one ferreted about in English or German books lent us by the Englishmen. Part of the time, at the request of the Captain, I occupied in writing my report of the fight. Kapitän v. Müller had already begun to put together all the news about the *Emden*. This was necessary, as our war log-book was burnt soon after the fight so that it should not get into the enemy's hands. One could while away many a weary hour with such official literature, and it was pleasant to return in thought to our gallant and beloved *Emden*. The return from this memory to the reality of captivity in an English transport was, however, always very bitter.

Every evening, at the salute of the colours, there was a concert by the regimental band of an Australian regiment. These men played very well, but in most cases only the latest English successes in which there was more noise than harmony. This change was welcome to the prisoners.

The arrival in Aden occurred on November 28th, but the transport only remained there a short time, which was employed in taking in coal and fresh water.

Then came the voyage through the Red Sea, which was "fine and warm," as a hot south wind had been blowing almost the whole voyage. Our next port was Suez, at the entrance to the canal of the same name. Variety was not lacking, for almost the whole time one can see the Arabian and African coasts.

On the way the news reached the ship that either in Suez or Port Said we were to be taken over by the armoured cruiser *Hampshire*, as the whole transport was to remain in Egypt.

At this the Englishmen cursed frightfully, as they would have been glad to spend some time in " old England." This was understandable, for most of these men had been in the colonies since their youth, and were therefore very anxious to get home. Through Turkey joining the German side, the original plans were altered. I am of the opinion that a large part of these men only enlisted in the hope of seeing home once again, for there was no general military service in England.

On our arrival in Suez a large number of our men, and the officers, were transferred to the *Hampshire*. Only we who were in the *Orvieto* were to remain in the transport till we reached Port Said.

The passage through the canal went smoothly, but we were locked up like criminals. We were not allowed on deck at all, and sentries were posted in front of our ports, armed to the teeth. The passage was, however, very interesting, as we could see all the fortifications of the English. They had already numbers of troops there, for the most part Sudanese and Indians. The whole length was like a fort. Trench followed trench, and battery followed battery. In my opinion an attack on the canal would only have been possible with a very large force.

The greater part of the passage was made in the night, so that our confinement was not so noticeable.

In the morning of December 2nd we arrived in Port Said. The *Hampshire* was already lying at the buoy. The harbour looked very full, with a large number of warships, and among them acquaintances from the East. The French armoured-cruisers *Montcalm* and *Duplex* were lying there, and a large number of troop-ships, torpedo-boats, minesweepers and patrol boats, hospital ships, and a few German ships which had been seized at the outbreak of war.

After the *Orvieto* had made fast, we also were removed to the *Hampshire*. All the passengers of the transport were at the railing to stare at our transfer, and naturally there were also innumerable cameras.

In the *Hampshire* we were received by Captain Grant, the captain of the cruiser, with great cordiality. It was noticeable at once that we were among members of our own profession. The whole tone was far warmer. That we were received so cordially by the *Hampshire* was especially remarkable, as this ship had been detailed to chase us. Captain Grant had carried out the search admirably, but our luck and his ill-luck had brought us safely through.

Our accommodation in the *Hampshire* was very

good indeed. The English captain had completely abandoned his cabin to us. We could go on deck at any time, which was very pleasant at sea and in good weather.

Our men were in the forecastle, and were also in very good quarters.

In Port Said we were given an opportunity to replenish our more than scanty wardrobes, especially with warm things for our probable voyage to cold and foggy England. We bought civilian clothes, and a warm coat for each of us. The men received warm English marine uniforms.

Another friendly action of Captain Grant was that he presented us with German and English books which he had bought specially for us a short time before.

The next morning the *Hampshire* put to sea. Good weather and a calm sea allowed us partly to forget our captivity.

Wireless messages were coming in daily about the war, which contained fascinating news for us. Thanks to the kindness and chivalry of Captain Grant we were given these messages to read. We thus heard the news of the victory of Spee's squadron over the English squadron at Coronel.

On December 4th we had a disappointment. A message was received from the War Office saying that the *Hampshire* was not to take us to England, but to Malta, where everything was already prepared for our reception.

The hope of getting to England, and thus not being too far from home, was removed at one stroke.

On Sunday, December 6th, the worst day of my life, we reached Malta. During the entrance to the great harbour we had to stay below, so that we should not learn the position of the mine barrier and of the entrance.

In the afternoon we were taken ashore. We officers were taken in a cart to the Verdala Barracks, where we were to spend the next long period. The men and the subordinate officers were separated from us and taken to Fort Salvatore.

The difference between navy and army met the eye and ear at once. The hearty friendship of our professional fellows was missing now. Coldness and hardness were already noticeable in the tone of the army officers.

Shortly after six o'clock we arrived at Verdala Barracks. The huge, heavy gates shut behind us and our captivity proper began.

CHAPTER XIV

PRISONERS of war! I think that most people, even those who have not been in the same position, can imagine a little what these words signify.

At Malta on the whole our treatment was tolerable. The Verdala Barracks proved to be the old fort barracks, and were about 218 to 240 yards long, and 44 yards wide. On the west front the building was continued at a right-angle, in a block 76 yards broad and 55 yards long. Our quarters were in the buildings opening on to the court thus formed.

Kapitän v. Müller was given a room to himself on an upper story, but we officers were divided between three rooms which were on the ground floor and next to each other.

In the first room were Kapitänleutnant Klöpper, Oberleutnant z. S. Witthoeft, Leutnant z. S. Schall, and I. In the second were Stabsarzt Dr. Luther and Marine-Oberingenieur Ellerbroek. In the third were Marine-Ingenieur Andresen, Leutnant z. S. Fikentscher, and Marine-Ingenieur Haas.

The English offered me a room to myself, but I refused for two reasons. I did not wish to be better lodged than my companions, and, secondly, we were of the opinion that the war would not last long, and that our captivity would therefore only be for a short period. In addition, I was firmly convinced that the English would make capital out of the special consideration, by stating that the treatment of all prisoners of war was good, and that the Prince of Hohenzollern had had a large room to himself.

The hope and the thought that we should be by ourselves at Malta were erroneous.

The gates had scarcely shut behind us when we were approached by a number of people, and we were at once asked if we were the *Emden's* officers. An affirmative called forth a storm of greetings from the civilian prisoners, consisting of shop-keepers and employees of hotels and of big firms in Egypt and at Malta. There was also a number of captains, officers and men of German and Austrian ships that had been captured. The English had also interned here nationalist Egyptians and Arabs, and pro-German Greeks. Anybody who did not forward English interests, or opposed them, was imprisoned. The English seized all without consideration. If in Germany and Austria we had imprisoned, at the beginning of the war, all suspicious persons, espionage would have been sooner brought to an end.

These civilian prisoners, who had heard a lot about the exploits of the *Emden*, gave us a great ovation. During the first few days of our captivity a singing club was founded, and a performance was given in the court-yard opposite the room of Kapitän v. Müller, ending with the National Hymn. This tribute was quite touching, many people having tears in their eyes.

The bitter feeling that one was a prisoner, and could no longer devote one's life and blood to the service of the Fatherland, was unspeakably painful. It was especially so for those who had not had an opportunity of fighting for the Fatherland.

There were, however, among the civilian prisoners some who were glad they had not been forced to fight. In isolated cases some prisoners expressed sympathy for the English, perhaps in the hope of being set free. Their hopes were, however, disappointed. The English despised such creatures, but made use of them as spies in the camp.

In the days following our painful entry into captivity we settled down in the rooms given us. To make the rooms inhabitable a number of articles had to be supplied. We then found out the disposition of the different camps. Our section was the Verdala Barracks, and adjoining it on the south was the main camp, the St. Clemens Camp. The men there were, with few exceptions, accommodated in tents, an example of the " humanity " of the English. In fine weather it was possible to endure the tents, but during rain or wind storms—the latter were very frequent—

19

these wretched prisoners had a miserable existence. Often at night they had to turn out to
secure the tents, which always broke away in a
storm. In severe rain, which was of a tropical
character, the whole tent was foot-deep in
water. Naturally this did not improve their
clothing.

The next prisoners' camp was the Polverista
Barracks, where at the beginning there were very
few prisoners. These barracks were specially
reserved for female prisoners, who could not be
put into the ordinary camps.

Finally, there was Fort San Salvatore, where
the *Emden's* subordinate officers and men were
accommodated. Only the officers' servants were
allowed to live in the Verdala Barracks.

At first no communication was allowed between
the different camps, but some time later limited
communication was permitted.

The lack of room for exercise was very much
felt, and increased the trial of our imprisonment.
We and 400 other prisoners had only the narrow
court-yard for exercise. Kapitän v. Müller brought
the complaint to the notice of the English com-
mander and asked for it to be remedied. This
demand was right, and easy to grant.

In the course of time a number of grievances
needing remedying made their appearance.
Complaints increased, and, to give the reader a
clear picture, the following manifesto was drawn
up :

I.—Provisions

(*a*) The fresh vegetables supplied by the Government are three-quarters uneatable, and have to be thrown away. The potatoes delivered are largely refuse. In autumn the potatoes delivered, both as to quantity and quality, give rise to various complaints every year. All complaints, although acknowledged by the English doctor, are in vain.

(*b*) The prisoners who cannot buy food with their own money are not supplied with sufficient food.

(*c*) The ship's company of *S.M.S. Breslau*, who are accommodated in Fort Salvatore, are cheated of a large portion of their proper allowance of food by the English soldiers.

II

A.—Accommodation in the Verdala Barracks.

(*a*) For three years we have been confined in rooms of which the windows opening outwards are boarded up.

(*b*) The court-yard and exercise place lie between high fortified walls. The exercise ground, which is insufficient, and commands no view of the distance, is always closed one hour before sunset, and we are thus deprived of any opportunity of taking the air during the cool time of the day. This is especially painful in summer, during the severe heat. The state of health during the third summer made it plain how much our resistance has suffered, and the prospect for the fourth summer is hopeless. A number of cases of madness and attempted suicide bear witness to the conditions. On a windy day it is impossible to stay in the court-yard because of the unbearable dust-clouds. The epidemic outbreaks of ear complaints apparently arise from this nuisance.

(c) There are no rooms for those who wish to read, study, practise gymnastics, etc.

(d) There is no room provided for Divine Service. The padres have to hold service in their bedrooms.

(e) There is a constant shortage of water. The bathrooms are completely inadequate, so that requests for baths have to be refused. There are only four warm baths among 650 men. These four baths cannot be used during the whole of the day. There are only about ninety baths a week. The charge for a warm bath is sixpence per person, so that the poorer prisoners cannot take them.

(f) The barracks are overfilled, and full of bugs. They hold 350 soldiers in peace-time, and there are now 650 men confined there.

B.—St. Clemens Camp.

850 men are here accommodated in astonishingly little space. The greater part have lived

for three and a half years three in a tent, the
diameter of which is just 4 yards 1 foot. The space
is so small in the camp that ten of these tents
have their openings 11 yards from the latrines
used by the whole 850 persons. For the day
and the evening there is only one room, which
is usually so crowded that a seat cannot be
obtained by each prisoner. During the long
winter evenings, when it is impossible to remain
in the tents on account of the cold, there are
five or six weak electric lamps for this room.
In addition, each man receives one small thin
candle weekly, which is burnt in a few hours.
There is no room for undisturbed study or reading. With some trouble we got a somewhat
larger tent for instruction purposes, but had
to supply furniture for it at our own cost. It
is a matter for wonder that almost a thousand
educated men, penned together like animals,
and unable to be alone even for a few minutes,
should have endured this martyrdom with so
few regrettable consequences.

The lack of water is, if possible, even greater
in St. Clemens Camp than in Verdala. In summer
there is often no water after nine o'clock. There
are only four baths in the whole camp, and only
one for warm baths. For 850 men ! A hot
bath costs sixpence. Even when the water is
most plentiful there are not more than eight
warm baths. The state of the latrines is
scandalous.

C.—

In Fort Salvatore 150 men of *S.M.S. Emden* spent three hopeless years in a fortified building surrounded and shut off from the world by high walls, without sufficient room for bodily exercise. They suffered severely from the lack of exercise and confinement, so that most of them were in a condition of irritability through illness. The part of the ship's company of *S.M.S Breslau* which was brought here is now quartered in these buildings.

D.—*Polverista.*

Here also the people are accommodated in space insufficient for exercise, more fitted for beasts than men. It is surprising that the great British Empire could not find more room for its prisoners.

III.—HOSPITAL

(*a*) The Cottonera Hospital (by this is to be understood only the prisoners' ward, for the hospital proper is very well equipped) has only one room for all sorts and stages of illness. This room is very primitively equipped (battered enamel vessels serve for eating and drinking vessels) and altogether unsuited for the treatment of severe cases. For convalescents, there was for a long time no arrangements for giving them any freedom. Only after repeated requests and representations was a space granted, of $7\frac{1}{2} \times 7\frac{1}{2}$ yards, surrounded by barbed wire.

(*b*) The roof of the hospital is not watertight, so that every time it rains the patients' beds get wet through.

(*c*) Convalescents are given neither special food nor special treatment. The food is quite insufficient for all patients, and quite without variety. Their fellow-prisoners have no opportunity to send in food, and the patients themselves cannot buy it.

(*d*) Treatment by specialists is not to be procured even if the patients are prepared to pay for it.

(*e*) Severe cases, and among them lung cases and paralysed cases, are not considered suitable for exchange, and when this is the case the patient is in such a hopeless condition that there is danger of his death. Many died here or on the way home in consequence of this treatment (Major Huber, Hoffmann, Dr. Breitenfeld, Sessler, Bruns), and others still here expect a like fate. The condition of the lung patients, in the Imtarsa, is particularly unsatisfactory (Tibelius, Molnar, Ali Hafiz). They complain of insufficient food, and, in addition, no account is taken of the state of the individual case. Our numerous attempts to bring about an improvement in their lot, or to get them sent home, or at least to be allowed to pay them a visit, met the impenetrable armour of military medical bureaucracy. It is often forbidden to send food, and when it is allowed it is impossible to carry it through.

The number of deaths up to March, 1918,
twenty-five. Died on the journey home, three.
Died soon after returning home, four. (For
madness and suicide, see II (*b*).)

IV.—TREATMENT OF THE CIVILIAN PRISONERS

(*a*) In spite of many representations the regula-
tions of the enemy government concerning civilian
prisoners were not disclosed to the prisoners.
There was therefore no possibility of finding out
how far civilian prisoners are bound to carry
out work both within and outside the camp.
When the civilian prisoners were forced to prepare
a camp for captured officers the authorities referred
to Article 42, and read this article out. This
article appears to us, however, to be insufficient
ground. An application by the Austrians to the
Swedish consul has not so far been answered.

Lately civilian prisoners have been ordered to
pitch tents outside the barbed wire for English
soldiers and men. When the prisoners refused
they received disciplinary punishment, and when
they still refused were threatened with twenty-
eight days in the military detention barracks, for
mutiny. Later this punishment was remitted,
" by grace," and each man was offered a—
glass of beer, in the name of the Commanding
Officer.

(*b*) The decisions under martial law are inhuman
(ten months' imprisonment for attempted flight)

and are not in accordance with the provisions of the Hague Convention.

(c) Walks are only allowed under strict guard of soldiers with fixed bayonets, and in large numbers.

V.—Post

(a) Letters are greatly delayed, and also money remittances, and the rate of exchange on money sent to us is falsified to our disadvantage. For 2,000 marks, which the Swedish Legation in London sent at Christmas, 1917, on behalf of the Red Cross, £60 instead of £81 was paid out.

(b) Letters are destroyed by the censor without the sender being informed.

VI.—Canteen

(a) The prices paid in the canteen are exorbitant, even in relation to the prices paid in Malta. By their monopoly of sales the prisoners are in the hands of the canteen staff. The keeper is indeed bound by regulation (Sec. 7.—The prices at which they are sold shall be at retail market prices, consistent with quality) to sell at market prices, but he never keeps to the regulation. There is no improvement in this situation in spite of the pressing representations that have been made.

(b) Repairs in the camp are paid, without

accounting, out of the canteen refund (discount), i.e. out of the money of the prisoners.

(c) The pumping of water for the prisoners is also paid for out of the refund.

VII.—MEDICAMENTS

Medicaments sent from home, particularly those in liquid form, even when they had been allowed by the doctor and certified necessary, are kept back for reasons that were not valid. There is a chronic lack of necessary medicaments and medical stores.

VIII.—DENTIST

Sufferers from toothache do not receive proper attention. There are only two dentists in the camp, an Austrian and a German. In spite of skill and good intentions, these dentists are often not in a position to help, on account of their youth and inexperience, and especially because of the lack of proper instruments. It is, however, almost impossible to get treatment by a good English dentist.

IX.—NEUTRAL REPRESENTATION

It is a drawback that there are no energetic neutral representatives on the spot. The correspondence with the Swedish consul here, a Maltese, leaves much to be desired. Requests and complaints to the Swedish Legation in London are without success in all cases of importance (unjust treatment of civilian prisoners). According to the Legation the English Government refuses to allow these complaints to be forwarded to the German Government, and refuses also to mitigate the injustice. To all other complaints no answer has been received.

It is necessary that all the camps here should be visited regularly, about once in six months, by a neutral commission, to which at least one doctor should be attached, and which should give an opportunity to those interned to make complaints.

MALTA, *March* 21st, 1918.

All communications with the English authorities were carried on through a special camp committee. These representatives of the prisoners had to present all complaints, etc., to the Commanding Officer of the camp. The refusal of requests, introduction of repairs, etc., all lay in the hands of this one man, who almost always gave the answer : " Well ! I will do my best ! " At first this friendly-sounding phrase pleased people, but later we learnt that it was an empty phrase, and that complaints were not remedied nor even mitigated.

A very evil characteristic of the English was that of corruptibility, the officers excepted. To achieve anything certainly one could go far, according to the rank of the person concerned,

with money or a bottle of whisky. By this
means certain persons were allowed, or at least
were not hindered, from going for walks even into
the town of Valetta. We officers regarded such
practices as corrupt, and renounced any favours
of this kind. In the beginning military control
was not sharp, and one could do or leave undone
what one liked in camp. This was altered when
Leutnant z. S. Fikentscher and an Austrian
civilian prisoner succeeded in escaping from the
camp and from Malta, and strict control was
imposed. Sentries were posted even on the roofs
of the barracks, whereas up to that time there had
been only Maltese guards round the camp.

I am convinced that the escape of Fikentschen
would not have been noticed if some degraded
creatures had not reported it to the English.

All privileges were withdrawn, as the English
Commandant regarded the escape as a personal
affront.

The feelings of the officers were very fine and
great, but they wished to be left in peace. They
abominated any disturbance of their dignity, and
rewarded any unpleasantness with a hail of
reprisals.

Immediately after the beginning of my captivity
I wrote a letter home, and expected an immediate
answer. I only received it, however, after three
and a half months. The English censor was to
blame for the delay. They were frightened of
" secret news " for me. A letter to my sister,

the Queen of Portugal, was likewise delayed. I could not understand this terrible anxiety of the English, for what could we have said about Malta ? In the first two years we never left the camp, and the windows opening on the town and harbour had been boarded up ! The object—of depriving us of a view of the naval harbour—was not, however, achieved, for we bored holes in the boards, and through them we could not only watch the harbour, but overlook some very interesting things. For instance, on one occasion, a hospital ship being loaded with ammunition boxes ! What we noticed specially about this hospital ship was that she was far below the loading mark in the water. This fact was very important, for it could be inferred that not only ammunition but also other war material was certainly stowed in her holds. This fact is naturally denied, but what one has oneself seen one can judge according to one's ability, especially if one happens to be a nautical officer and acquainted with the loading capacity of a ship.

The loopholes we had bored provided plenty of variety, especially while the English were engaged in the Dardanelles. Transports filled with soldiers came in daily, and warships of all sizes made fast in the harbour to coal or provision.

Our first Christmas passed very dismally. We had no news from home, and did not know what losses the war had inflicted on our families.

In the course of the summer of 1915 a novelty

was introduced, and our hitherto very narrow space for exercise was enlarged. South of the barracks lay the old Fort Glacis, sparsely covered with grass, and possessing a path of 219 yards, where we were permitted to walk. We erected a skittle-alley at once, which provided us with much pleasure and amusement. Fort Glacis was soon pulled down, and on the space thus provided gardens were raised, with huts and green things. This work gave me much pleasure, if only for the opportunity of physical labour.

In the course of time we were also permitted to go into St. Clemens Camp during certain hours. Within these hours a certain number of prisoners from St. Clemens could visit Verdala, and vice versa.

The camp orchestra, led by a very capable conductor, gave pleasure by its performances.

On the birthdays of our Kaiser Wilhelm and of the Austrian Kaiser Franz Joseph, and after his death that of Kaiser Karl, we were able, with the permission of the English authorities, to hold certain festivities and to decorate the barracks with flags, which was friendly of the Englishmen, in view of the fact that it was impossible to see into the camp from the town.

The accommodation of cases of illness was very bad in this first year of our captivity. If a prisoner was sick he had to appear before the camp doctor, who appeared every day in a certain place. Some of these doctors were very friendly, but there were also the " roughlegs " who hoped by their " roughleggedness " to conceal their lack of skill, etc. If it was impossible to treat them in camp the patients were consigned to Cottonera Hospital—there was a special building for prisoners. This was a former store-shed which had been " adapted " for prisoners. The treatment of patients was carried out by Sisters of the Red Cross. The sanitary measures defy description. For example, the following case was told me. As there was only one room provided, venereal cases lay next to other patients. The meals were served on tin plates, and it repeatedly happened that an ordinary patient had to eat from the plate previously used by a venereal case. This was for a long time the cause of many complaints by our camp committee before it was changed.

Our neutral representative was the consul of the United States of America in Valetta, but we could not do much through this man, whose own interests came first. We gladly renounced his assistance, for definite results of any importance were hardly ever achieved by him. Later the Swedish consul, who was a Maltese, received the representation for the Swedish Legation in London. I, personally, had much to do with this man, and in the course of time achieved much, but he also was not completely free in his dealings, for he was a merchant and dependent on the favour of the English authorities.

I would like to treat here of a very interesting legal point. According to international law, doctors, first-aid staff, and priests, in so far as they have not actively used weapons, are considered free—that is, they may not be treated as prisoners of war. In spite of this international agreement the English authorities interned several doctors from merchant-ships in Malta for a long time, as well as our doctor from the *Emden*, Stabsarzt Dr. Luther. It was only after long correspondence that they were set free.

Two Franciscan Fathers, who at the beginning of the war were stationed in Alexandria for convalescence, were arrested on suspicion of espionage, and later brought to Malta, where both the unfortunate men had to remain till the close of our captivity. All attempts to effect their release, both consular and ecclesiastical, failed. Their stay in the camp was very welcome to the Catholics, as it rendered possible the celebration of Holy Mass on Sundays and holy days, but one was sorry for the two worthy gentlemen, who were not in their first youth.

After every attempt had been made to have them set free, or at least accommodated in some Maltese cloister, the request was put forward that at least a proper room might be furnished for the celebration of Divine Service, but this request also fell on unfruitful ground. The two priests had to read Mass in the same room that they

passed the night in. These facts are speaking
witnesses for the " humanity " of the camp
authorities, in this case the War Office.

I found an opportunity of laying this matter
before the Archbishop of Malta, who completely
agreed, and promised me his help, but emphasised
that only the War Office could make the decision.
I am firmly convinced that the Archbishop did
his utmost, but without result.

Those of the prisoners who had no money were
in a bad condition. Societies were formed in the
various camps to provide underclothes and small
things for these men. In 1915 the " German-
Austro-Hungarian Charitable Union " was formed
as central authority for this work, and Kapitän
v. Müller was chosen as President. Later the
Turkish Charitable Union also joined up.

Our union got into communication with the
Red Cross of the respective countries, and begged
for more frequent remittances of money and gifts.
The union succeeded in keeping a number of our
fellow-prisoners for the five years of their tribula-
tion. A very necessary understanding was arrived
at with the English authorities, for among the
2,000 prisoners there were some who took every
opportunity of getting hold of money. Through
this understanding the respective treasurers were
enabled to control the sums of money sent for
prisoners. If someone came with a request for
assistance his case was examined, and if it was
found from the post-book that he had received

20

money, and was completely provided with the necessaries of life, his request was refused.

Kapitän v. Müller was very active in this matter and in that of camp complaints, which must have been very unwelcome to the authorities, for in 1917, without any warning, he was removed from Malta and taken to England. The procedure was as follows : One day Kapitän v. Müller was ordered to go to the Governor of Malta. As this was a frequent request we had no suspicions, but several hours passed and our Captain did not return. To us officers of the *Emden* the interval was full of suspense. We went to his room and removed all reports and writings which it was not desirable to allow to fall into the hands of the English. Soon afterwards an officer of the camp authorities came to make a search, but naturally he found nothing.

In the meantime Kapitän v. Müller had gone to the Governor and received from him the news that he was that day to be sent to England. Permission to return to the camp was refused. His scanty possessions would " follow." This theatrical mystery speaks volumes for itself.

Thus we were deprived of our Captain, and with him we lost at the same time the representative of our camp and the President of the Charitable Union. I was chosen as his successor in the latter post, and I accepted readily that position, as one could do much good. I remained President till the end of our captivity at Malta.

"EMDEN" RUN AGROUND

After the removal of our Captain the responsibility for the *Emden's* men was taken over by Oberleutnant z. S. Witthoeft. He occupied this post till the end of our imprisonment and showed great activity.

In the course of time some improvement was granted in the opportunity for intercourse between the camps. Thus, for instance, we officers were permitted to go to Fort Salvatore at Christmas and on similar occasions. This permission was interdependent of the agreement arrived at by Germany and England in August, 1916, by which prisoners of war were to be allowed to take walks outside the prison camps. At first they demanded our word of honour that we would make no attempts to escape during these walks, or that we would make no preparations for such attempts, but as we would not give this undertaking we had to forgo this liberty. When, however, our military authorities had given permission, there was no longer any reason against giving our words of honour.

These walks brought welcome variety into our monotonous lives. Although the place is stony and ugly there was now some possibility of a view of the distance, which was the more refreshing because some of the prisoners had completely ruined their eyes by staring at the camp walls. These walks took place twice weekly, and each lasted for two hours. The German officers were accompanied by an English or Maltese officer and a man without arms. With the rest of the prisoners it was otherwise, as they had not to give their word of honour and had to walk in groups of 100–150 men. These groups were guarded by from 20–30 fully-armed men and an English officer.

From the year 1917 onwards we were allowed a further favour in being permitted to bathe, in summer, in the Marsa Skala Bay. It was wonderfully refreshing to feel the sea again, but the pleasure was somewhat damped by the restriction as to time. We were only permitted to remain on the beach for half an hour !

Much depended on the English officer who accompanied us. Most of them were friendly and companionable, and patient enough to talk politics. Many verbal battles took place, each giving as good as he got.

During my five years' imprisonment at Malta I had to go to hospital three times for illness. The first two times I was sent to the Cottonera Hospital. It must be said that the accommodation and care of officers was very good I always had a room to myself. The Sisters took all possible trouble to lighten the lot of the patients, and so did some of the doctors, in particular one Scotchman who had studied in Germany. He accompanied me on my walks as convalescent, and did not too anxiously observe the marching orders. The third and last time I went sick I had influenza, which at that time, in 1918, was very rife at Malta. I went to the Imtarsa Hospital. This epidemic was very severe among the prisoners, eighty per cent. of whom caught it, which was not surprising in the crowded space.

This disease raged at the same time all over the island, and presented a colossal task to the English Red Cross, which was, however, well carried out.

It is necessary to say here that in the course of time the conditions of health improved.

In 1918, an increase occurred in the number of prisoners owing to the arrival of men from the *Breslau* and officers and men from East Africa. They were accommodated in a special camp near Polverista, and we had lively communications with them.

The worst blow of all in our long and severe imprisonment was the news of the revolution in Germany.

When, in November, 1918, I read the telegram of Reuter's bureau concerning the revolution in Munich, I would not believe it, and thought it all false, but I was soon convinced of the incredible truth. For a whole day I locked myself into my room. I had to be alone at this news of faithlessness and revolution at home.

Of course there were some among the prisoners who were Socialist, and who short-sightedly rejoiced at the revolution. They conducted themselves towards me, however, as politely as formerly.

The greatest joy at the revolution was to be found among the English, for which one could not blame them. If the case had been reversed we should not have wept.

What somewhat mitigated the news for us at Malta was the hope that we should now soon be allowed to go home, for the armistice was soon signed. We could hope to our hearts' content, but we could not leave Malta. Our patience was put to a severe test. The English comforted us by speaking of the Peace Treaty, but that also came and still there was not the least prospect of release from our captivity.

Rage possessed us.

Our anger led us at first to hunger-strikes, which did not impress the English, but it was otherwise with the nightly " concerts," composed of frightful cat-like serenades, which raised a fearful noise. By agreement a din was made at midnight by all the camps drumming on their tin utensils and pails. At the same time the enraged prisoners howled loudly enough to soften the stones. The noise was so frightful that there can be no conception of it. It defies description, and reminded one of madness. It carried far out over the town of Valetta, robbing the Maltese of sleep and leading to furious complaints.

Little success attended this " concert of rage," for only in November, 1919, did a few prisoners receive permission to sail for Germany, at their own expense. The reason was that the ship which was to take home the whole of the prisoners was on her way, and therefore we had to wait.

During this bitter time of waiting, troops commanded by General Liman v. Sanders arrived at Malta from Constantinople. These troops were to be taken to Hamburg, for they were free— that is, they were allowed to return home unhindered. In spite of this Excellenz von Sanders was stopped, and fetched from his ship to speak to the Governor of Malta. No interview, however, took place. The German General, who had been guaranteed free conduct, was taken prisoner! This was entirely arbitrary on the part of the English, for there was no ground for such a breach of faith.

Liman von Sanders was at first confined in a barrack by himself, and later in the camp with the East African officers, and was for some time treated as a prisoner. He was only liberated after many protests.

The prisoners were still not taken home. Apparently the new Republican Government was lacking in energy.

The English put no difficulties in the way of travelling home at one's own expense. Some prisoners, therefore, raked together their last few pence and undertook the journey in spite of the privations involved.

The hour of my release struck on November 12th, 1919, in the afternoon. I gave my word, and kept it, to take decisive steps on behalf of the

comrades I had left behind. Accordingly, by
Christmas of the same year all the German,
Austrian, and Hungarian prisoners from Malta
were at home with their relations.

In the evening of November 12th, 1919, I
steamed away from Malta, together with Count
Bernhard v. Matuschka, who had fought under
Lettow-Vorbeck in German East Africa.

I cannot describe, and can hardly suggest, how
great a joy it was to be free again. Five of the
best years of my youth, five bitter years as a
prisoner of war, were ended.

We went from Malta to Syracuse in an Italian
ship, which entered the harbour of Syracuse early
in the morning of November 13th. From there
we went by railway, via Messina and Naples, to
Rome, where a few formalities had to be gone
through.

On the evening of the 14th we went cheerfully
forward to Milan, and on the morning of the
15th to Zürich, where we paused "to get our
breath" for thirty-six hours.

We proceeded on the 17th to Constance, where
we arrived in the afternoon, and my father was
waiting for me. On account of the bad connec-
tion we had to sleep the night in Constance. At
nine in the morning of November 18th we at last
arrived safely at my beloved home, Sigmaringen.

For full five years—a great, thrilling, but also
an oppressive time—I had fought honourably and
dutifully for the Fatherland. I sacrificed the best

years of my life, endured and suffered bitterly, and lost what is irrecoverable. Nevertheless, I would not be without the memory, and would wish to preserve to my last breath the inspiring feeling of having faithfully served the honour and fame of the Fatherland in S.M. Ship *Emden*.

THE END

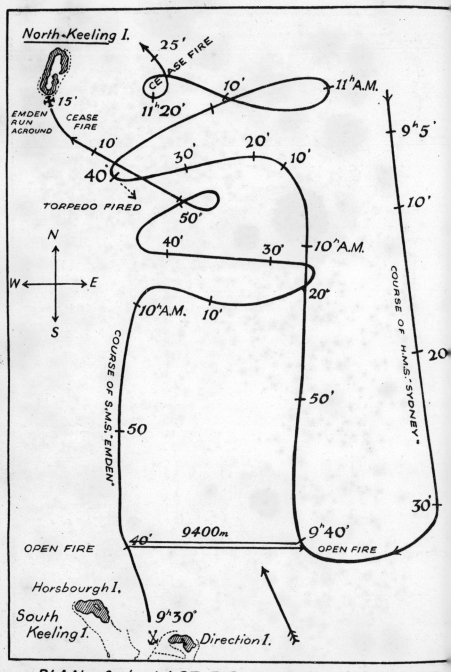

PLAN of the LAST FIGHT; "EMDEN" v "SYDNEY".